Fellowships in International Affairs

Fellowships in International Affairs

∎

A Guide to Opportunities in the United States and Abroad

WOMEN IN INTERNATIONAL SECURITY

LYNNE
RIENNER
PUBLISHERS

BOULDER
LONDON

JX
1293
.U6
F39
1994

Published in the United States of America in 1994 by
Lynne Rienner Publishers, Inc.
1800 30th Street, Boulder, Colorado 80301

and in the United Kingdom by
Lynne Rienner Publishers, Inc.
3 Henrietta Street, Covent Garden, London WC2E 8LU

© 1994 by Women In International Security. All rights reserved

Library of Congress Cataloging-in-Publication Data
Fellowships in international affairs : a guide to opportunities in the
United States and abroad / Women in International Security.
    p. cm.
    This directory evolved from a series of workshops held during the
WIIS Summer Symposia on International Security, 1990–1993.
    Includes bibliographical references and index.
    ISBN 1-55587-517-3 (pbk. : acid-free paper)
    1. International Relations—Study and teaching—United States—
Directories. 2. International Relations—Scholarships,
fellowships, etc.—Directories. I. Women in International Security
(Project)
JX1293.U6F39   1994   94-4468
378.3'3'025—dc20   CIP

British Cataloguing in Publication Data
A Cataloguing in Publication record for this book
is available from the British Library.

Printed and bound in the United States of America

∞ The paper used in this publication meets the requirements
of the American National Standard for Permanence of
Paper for Printed Library Materials Z39.48-1984.

Contents

Preface	vii
Acknowledgments	ix
About This Directory	xi
The Fellowships	1
Appendixes	145
On the Art of Writing Proposals: Some Candid Suggestions for Applicants to Social Science Research Council Competitions, *Adam Przeworski and Frank Salomon*	147
Sample Curriculum Vitae	155
Sample Cover Letter	157
Selected Bibliography of Other Fellowship Directories	159
Indexes	161
Fellowships by Title	163
Granting Organizations by Geographic Area of Specialization or Location	171
Granting Organizations by Fellowship Type	177
About Women In International Security	189
About the Center for International and Security Studies at Maryland	193
Fellowship Update Form	195

Preface

The Women In International Security (WIIS) *Fellowships in International Affairs: A Guide to Opportunities in the United States and Abroad* evolved from a series of workshops held during the WIIS Summer Symposia on International Security from 1990 to 1993. The workshop has now become a permanent part of each symposium, and although optional, it has always been a well-attended informal discussion session addressing the importance of professional development through research support and, we hope, consequent publication. The workshops have been designed to acquaint symposium participants with the opportunities available to them in pursuing their research and studies.

Having compiled substantial materials on grants and fellowships over a period of four years, WIIS decided to make the information more widely available. We do this in the hope that the grants are viewed as one aspect of developing a career in international security. So often, individuals are discouraged from applying for support because they doubt that they are sufficiently qualified or that the conditions of the grants are appropriate to the research they are pursuing. WIIS attempts in this publication to clarify at least the minimum qualifications for the grants, the basic conditions of the offerings, and both the more traditional and the lesser-known opportunities. In so doing, we hope to benefit U.S. and international students and researchers and provide possible suggestions for further investigation into alternative funding support. We encourage those who do not find the correct "fit" in this directory to call the funding sources listed here, use some of the directories listed at the back, and be persistent but flexible in searching for appropriate support.

Though they may seem obvious, several suggestions that have been discussed in the WIIS workshops are helpful to bear in mind as you use this directory. One, give close attention to the development of the proposal and do any necessary background research for your submission. Two, seek advice and assistance from faculty or experienced experts within your own institution. Three, be familiar with the scholars in the field, including the foreign scholars if research abroad is necessary or desirable; depending on the stage in your research, this might include seeking contact with the appropriate scholars and requesting their response to your ideas. Four, take full advantage of opportunities to present and discuss your work in its later stages at conferences and other forums. Five, take any opportunity to publish your research; this will both challenge and sharpen your arguments and provide interested funders with evidence of your commitment to the field and topic area. Finally, keep in mind that even if you are not successful with a particular application, you may still heighten your chances of success in another competition or establish your name as a serious scholar within the field.

On behalf of WIIS, I would like to express my thanks to all who contributed to this directory. First and foremost, the students at the symposia gave very helpful insights into the application processes, their own experiences, and sources for the directory. Second, the comments and additions made by WIIS president Catherine McArdle Kelleher and members of the WIIS boards were extremely valuable. In particular, the Summer Symposium Committee composed of Yvonne Bartoli, Ellen Blalock, Natalie Goldring, Jo Husbands, and Patricia Stein Wrightson provided unending advice and support for the symposia generally and the directory specifically. Sincere thanks also go to the current and former executive directors of WIIS, Carola Weil and Frances G. Burwell.

Gale A. Mattox
Chair
Summer Symposium Committee

Acknowledgments

This directory would not have been possible without the support and assistance of many individuals and institutions. Numerous graduate students, scholars, and professionals around the world contributed suggestions and useful ideas. Our special appreciation goes to WIIS summer intern Jennifer Zaslow, who spent long hours gathering, entering into the computer, updating, and editing all the information. Rosalind Reynolds and Rachel Vanlandingham, MacArthur scholars at the Center for International and Security Studies at the University of Maryland (CISSM), and WIIS interns Patricia Hearn and Chris Martin contributed valuable time and effort. Dana Sample, WIIS program coordinator, provided crucial oversight and assistance at every step of the project.

Many others not directly involved in this WIIS project contributed significantly to its existence and completion. The students, faculty, and staff of CISSM, under the auspices of Director I. M. Destler, have been most encouraging. Dean Michael Nacht, faculty, and staff of the School of Public Affairs at the University of Maryland continue to provide WIIS with a supportive environment. The McKeldin Graduate Library and the Fellowship Office of the University of Maryland at College Park provided valuable reference sources and access to the Illinois Researcher Information System, a database of financial assistance opportunities. Representatives of the diplomatic community based in Washington, D.C., the Institute of International Education (IIE), UN-affiliated organizations, and research organizations such as the Social Science Research Council (SSRC) were also most helpful.

The Ford Foundation, by providing financial support for WIIS, supplied essential assistance to this fellowship directory. We are also grateful to the Carnegie Corporation of New York for providing the funds to conduct the WIIS annual Summer Symposia for graduate students, which served as the primary impetus for this directory.

WIIS Advisory and Executive Board members deserve special recognition for their show of strong support and enthusiasm for the Summer Symposia. Going well beyond the call of duty, board members have devoted tremendous time and energy to making the Summer Symposia a success.

Finally, special thanks go to Gale A. Mattox, vice president of WIIS and chair of the WIIS Summer Symposium Committee. With an unwavering commitment to the advancement of women just entering the field of international security studies, Professor Mattox has been a crucial factor in the success of the Summer Symposium each year. Indeed, this volume was undertaken at her initiative and has proceeded under her direction; it is a direct outcome of her Summer Symposium workshop on grants and fellowships.

Catherine M. Kelleher
President
WIIS

Carola Weil
Executive Director
WIIS

About This Directory

The entries compiled in this directory are derived from several different sources, including fellowship and grant guidebooks, computerized databases, academic journals, and newsletters. WIIS also relied on suggestions by individual scholars and students. Finally, WIIS directly contacted and verified known grant-making organizations for information.

In beginning your own fellowship search, use this directory as a launching pad. We have organized the fellowships alphabetically by granting organization. All listings provide a brief description of the fellowship or grant, any qualifications required, and an address to contact for further information. Additional information—the stipend amount, duration of the fellowship, application procedures, deadlines—is included as available. Entries for organizations offering more than one type of fellowship include subheadings for each fellowship or grant.

To assist you further we have cross-referenced the entries in three indexes. The first lists fellowship titles and will assist you in identifying the organization that administers a specific grant or fellowship. If you are interested in support for research in or about a particular country or region, the second index will direct you to the appropriate granting organizations. The third index lists granting organizations by type and level of academic or career qualification supported by a particular fellowship or grant; thus, if you are interested specifically in support to complete your dissertation, or are looking for funding opportunities at a later stage in your career, this index will be especially helpful.

Please note that WIIS cannot assure all dates and terms of awards and grants. Always personally contact the organizations for the most current and complete information, and to ensure that the fellowships are still being offered and that the qualifications and deadlines have not changed. Consult your university library and fellowship office for additional guides to financial opportunities at the graduate, postgraduate, and more advanced levels. A selected bibliography of other fellowship guides is located in the appendix section for your convenience. The essay by Adam Przeworski and Frank Salomon, "On the Art of Writing Proposals," offers some useful guidelines for applying for the fellowships you select. A sample curriculum vitae and cover letter are also included to help refine your application.

Because it is impossible to be all-inclusive, we welcome corrections and additions for future, revised editions. A form for this purpose is at the back of the directory. For those interested in internships, see an earlier WIIS publication, *Internships for Women (and Men) in Foreign and Defense Policy,* published by Seven Locks Press.

THE FELLOWSHIPS

Konrad Adenauer Foundation

Research fellowships are awarded to German nationals. For more information contact the foundation office in Germany.

contact: Konrad Adenauer Foundation
Rathausallee 12
53757 St. Augustin/Germany
(49-0-2241) 246-0

American Association of University Women (AAUW) Educational Foundation

American Fellowships

The organization emphasizes a commitment to helping women through service in their community, profession, and field of research. The fellowship program supports dissertation and post-doctoral work.

qualifications: U.S. citizenship or permanent residency

duration: July 1 to June 30

stipend: Varies according to the academic level of the fellowship. Dissertation fellows: $13,500 for the yearlong fellowships; postdoctoral fellows: $20,000 to $25,000

deadline: Mid-November

applications available: August 1 to November 1

contact: AAUW Educational Foundation
1111 Sixteenth Street, NW
Washington, DC 20036-4873/USA
(202) 728-7603

International Fellowships

The fellowships provide for full-time graduate or postgraduate research in the United States by a non–U.S. citizen.

qualifications: Bachelor's degree

duration: September 1 to May 31

stipend: $14,000 for the academic year

deadline: December 1

applications available: July 15 to November 16

contact: See address above

Selected Professions Fellowships

Two fellowships are sponsored, one emphasizing science and technology at the master's level and the other awarded to a minority applicant pursuing a career in business administration, law, or medicine.

duration:	July 1 to June 30
stipend:	$5,000 to $9,500; a fellowship with a stipend of $13,500 is also offered to an engineering doctoral candidate to write a dissertation
deadline:	Mid-November
applications available:	August 1 to November 1
contact:	See address above

American Council of Learned Societies (ACLS)

Fellowships/Grants-in-Aid

The fellowships are offered for postdoctoral research in the humanities and humanities-related social sciences.

qualifications: U.S. citizenship or permanent residency, with a Ph.D. or equivalent scholarly experience obtained prior to application submission. Any previous "supported research leave" must have concluded five or more years prior to the application for the fellowship.

duration: Two to twelve months, beginning between July 1 and the subsequent February 1

stipend: $5,000 to $20,000

deadline: September 30

contact: Office of Fellowships and Grants
American Council of Learned Societies
228 East Forty-fifth Street
New York, NY 10017-3398/USA

ACLS Area Programs

See Social Science Research Council

American Defense Institute (ADI)

Fellowship in National Security Studies

Fellowships provide an opportunity for graduate and Ph.D. candidates interested in national security to work full time within the U.S. government. Fellows work in two to three internships in various parts of the government, including various bureaus as well as the congressional and White House staffs. ADI provides financial support enabling fellows to work for the U.S. defense establishment as unpaid student research assistants.

qualifications:	Enrollment in an M.A. or Ph.D program
deadline:	Mid-January
contact:	American Defense Institute 1055 North Fairfax Street, Second Floor Alexandria, VA 22314/USA (703) 519-7000

American Institute for Contemporary German Studies (AICGS)

DAAD (German Academic Exchange Service)- AICGS Summer Grant

The grant provides an opportunity to undertake research at AICGS in Washington, D.C.

qualifications:	Ph.D. candidate or recent Ph.D. recipient (degree received within the two years prior to application) or junior faculty member
duration:	One summer month (July or August)
contact:	Assistant to the Research Director AICGS 11 Dupont Circle, NW, Suite 350 Washington, DC 20036/USA (202) 332-9312

AICGS/DHI (German Historical Institute) Fellowships in Postwar German History

Resident research fellowships are available for U.S. and German historians and political scientists specializing in post–World War II Germany, especially the period between 1945 and 1955.

qualifications: Three fellowships are offered: one postdoctoral, one junior faculty, and one senior faculty

duration: One year

contact: See address above

The Bosch Younger Scholar Program in the Social Sciences

These fellowships assist postdoctoral students in transforming their dissertations into book manuscripts. The program is for a six- to twelve-month period, with the completion of the manuscript expected at the end of the fellowship.

contact: See address above

American Institute for Maghrib Studies, Johns Hopkins University

Small Grants Program

Grants are awarded to support research in North Africa or related areas.

qualifications: Graduate students, postdoctoral scholars, and professionals who are connected with a U.S. or Canadian university

duration: One to three months of research

stipend: $2,000

deadline: March 1

contact: Dr. William Zartman
School of Advanced International Studies
Johns Hopkins University
1740 Massachusetts Avenue, NW
Washington, DC 20036/USA
(202) 663-5680
FAX: (202) 663-5639

American Institute of Indian Studies (AIIS)

Senior (Postdoctoral) Research Fellowships

Fellowships are awarded to academic specialists in Indian studies. While in India, each senior research fellow is formally affiliated with an Indian university.

qualifications:	Doctoral degree or its equivalent, preferably within the humanities. After approval by the AIIS, all research programs must be approved by the government of India. U.S. citizens are eligible for AIIS grants, as are foreign nationals enrolled or teaching full time at U.S. colleges or universities.
duration:	Up to nine months
deadline:	July 1, for spring or summer of the following year
contact:	American Institute of Indian Studies 1130 East Fifty-ninth Street Chicago, IL 60637/USA (312) 702-8638

Fellowships for Senior Scholarly Development

Fellowships are offered to established scholars who have not previously specialized in Indian studies and to established professionals who have not previously worked or studied in India. Proposals in this second category should have a substantial research or project component, and the anticipated results should be clearly defined. While in India, each fellow will be formally affiliated with an Indian university.

qualifications:	U.S. citizenship or, for foreign nationals, enrollment or full-time teaching position at a U.S. college or university
duration:	Six to nine months
deadline:	July 1; awards announced in spring or summer of the following year
contact:	See address above

Junior (Dissertation) Fellowships

Fellowships are awarded to graduate students from all academic disciplines whose dissertation research requires study in India. Junior fellows have formal affiliation with Indian universities and Indian research supervisors.

qualifications:	Graduate students preparing for their dissertations
duration:	Up to eleven months
deadline:	July 1; awards announced in spring or summer of the following year
contact:	See address above

American Institute of Pakistan Studies (AIPS)

Fellowship Programs

The AIPS offers fellowships for predoctoral and postdoctoral candidates pursuing research in the social sciences or humanities with relevance to Pakistan. Length and timing of the awards are designed to meet individual needs.

qualifications:	U.S. or Canadian citizenship; completion of all course work for the doctorate
duration:	Two to nine months
stipend:	Maintenance allowance, travel, and other benefits
deadline:	January 1; awards announced in April
contact:	American Institute of Pakistan Studies P.O. Box 7568 Wake Forest University Winston-Salem, NC 27109/USA (919) 759-5449 or (919) 759-5453 FAX: (919) 759-6104

American Political Science Association (APSA)

APSA is the major professional organization in the United States for those engaged in the study of politics. APSA facilitates teaching and research on the U.S. political system.

Congressional Fellowship Program: Communications

This program sponsors eight political scientists and journalists to work closely with members of Congress as legislative aides. Fellows also attend seminars and lectures by experts in the policymaking process.

qualifications:	U.S. citizens and foreign nationals who have completed a Ph.D. within the fifteen years prior to application or have a bachelor's degree and a minimum of two years' full-time experience in the media
duration:	One year
stipend:	$24,000 plus a travel allowance
deadline:	October 1 to December 1
contact:	American Political Science Association MCI Communications Fellowships c/o Director, Congressional Fellowship Program American Political Science Association 1527 New Hampshire Avenue, NW Washington, DC 20036/USA (202) 483-2512

Congressional Fellowship Program: Federal Executives

This program offers senior-level federal executives the opportunity to participate directly in the legislative process. Fellows do not receive a stipend from APSA but continue to receive their regular salaries from their government agencies.

qualifications:	GS-13 or equivalent with a minimum of two years of federal service in the executive branch
duration:	One year
deadline:	October 1 to December 1
contact:	Congressional Fellowship Program American Political Science Association 1527 New Hampshire Avenue, NW Washington, DC 20036/USA (202) 483-2512

Congressional Fellowship Program: Political Science

This program offers political scientists in the early or middle stages of their careers the opportunity to participate directly in the legislative process.

qualifications:	Ph.D. within the fifteen years prior to application
duration:	December to August
stipend:	$26,000 plus a travel allowance
deadline:	December 15
contact:	See address above

Joan Shorenstein Barone Congressional Fellowship

This program offers broadcast journalists the opportunity to participate directly in the legislative process.

qualifications:	Bachelor's degree and two to ten years' full-time professional experience in radio or television reporting, on the air or as producer, director, writer, or researcher
stipend:	$26,000 plus a travel allowance
deadline:	December 15
contact:	See address above

The Robert Wood Johnson Health Policy Fellowship

This program provides midcareer health professionals with a better understanding of major issues in health policy and insight into how health programs are established.

qualifications:	Midcareer health professional working in academia
duration:	September through August
stipend:	$5,000
deadline:	Mid-November
contact:	Robert Wood Johnson Health Policy Fellows Institute of Medicine National Academy of Sciences Washington, DC 20418/USA (202) 334-1506

American Research Center in Egypt, Inc. (ARCE)

ARCE Fellowships

ARCE supports fellowships for U.S. scholars and students to conduct research into all periods and all phases of Egyptian civilization. While ARCE's primary emphases are cultural and archaeological, the organization also encourages research in the humanities and social sciences. Its broad aims are to obtain a fresh and more profound knowledge of Egypt and the Near East through scholarly research; to train U.S. specialists in Middle Eastern studies in academic disciplines that require familiarity with Egypt; to disseminate knowledge of Egypt and thus understanding of the whole Near East; and to promote U.S.-Egyptian cultural relations.

qualifications: Doctoral student or postdoctoral scholar; U.S. citizenship required for dissertational scholarships

duration: Between three and twelve months, the recipient to be in residence in Egypt for the course of the fellowship

stipend: Students: $1,000 per month; full professors: $2,300 per month; plus additional allowances for family members

deadline: November 1

contact: American Research Center in Egypt, Inc.
Hagop Kevorian Center for Near Eastern Studies
New York University
50 Washington Square South
New York, NY 10012/USA
(212) 998-8890

American-Scandinavian Foundation (ASF)

Fellowships and Grants for Study and Research

The ASF sponsors grants and fellowships to support U.S. citizens involved in advanced study and research in Denmark, Finland, Iceland, Norway, or Sweden.

qualifications: U.S. citizenship or permanent residency; bachelor's degree; competence in the language of the target country. Proposals may be in any field of study; other factors being equal, priority will be given to candidates at the dissertation level. Candidates are expected to have undertaken appropriate correspondence with institutions and scholars in Scandinavia.

stipend: Grants of $2,500; fellowships of $15,000

deadline: November 1

contact: The American-Scandinavian Foundation
Exchange Division
725 Park Avenue
New York, NY 10021/USA
(212) 879-9779

Citizens of Scandinavian countries interested in programs of study or research in the United States should contact one of the organizations below.

The Denmark-America
 Foundation
Dr. Tvaergade 44
1302 Copenhagen K/Denmark

League of Finnish-American
 Societies
Mechelininkatu 10
SF-001 00 Helsinki/Finland

The Icelandic-American Society
P.O. Box 7051
Reykjavik/Iceland

The Norway-America
 Association
Drammensveien 20 C
0255 Oslo 2/Norway

The Sweden-America
 Foundation
Box 5280
S-102 46
 Stockholm/Sweden

American University in Cairo (AUC)

African Graduate Fellowships

Each year the AUC provides up to ten fellowships to students throughout sub-Saharan Africa.

qualifications:	Student from sub-Saharan Africa
stipend:	Tuition fees for any of AUC's twelve master's degree programs
deadline:	March 1
contact:	International Graduate Program Coordinator Office of Provost American University in Cairo P.O. Box 2511 Cairo/Egypt (20-2) 357-6922 FAX 20-2-355-7565

Arms Control and Disarmament Agency (ACDA), U.S.

Hubert H. Humphrey Doctoral Fellowship

This fellowship is for Ph.D. students who are writing their dissertations. Research proposals should be designed to improve the understanding of current and future arms control and disarmament issues. The fellow must submit quarterly progress reports and a copy of the dissertation when completed and approved by the academic institution.

qualifications: Citizens or nationals of the United States who have completed all requirements for their doctorates except the dissertations. J.D. candidates are also eligible under certain conditions.

duration: Twelve months

stipend: $5,000 plus $3,400 toward tuition and fees at the graduate institution with which the fellow is affiliated

deadline: Mid-March, with fellowship beginning in either September or January

contact: Hubert H. Humphrey
  Doctoral Fellowship Program
Operations Analysis, Room 5726
U.S. Arms Control and Disarmament Agency
320 Twenty-first Street, NW
Washington, DC 20451/USA
(202) 647-4695

Asian Foundation

Asian Foundation Fellowships

The Asian Foundation funds high-level, English-speaking civil servants and other professionals from Asian countries to participate in the American Political Science Association (APSA) programs (see entry above for APSA).

qualifications: Asian citizenship with government experience and fluency in English

contact: The Asia Foundation
P.O. Box 3223
San Francisco, CA 94119/USA
(415) 982-4640

Association of African Universities

Staff Exchange Program

Staff Exchange Programs allow members of African universities to work at another university within Africa.

qualifications: Faculty affiliation at an African university

stipend: Travel expenses and/or an honorarium

deadline: None

contact: Association of African Universities
P.O. Box 5744
Accra-North/Ghana

Association of Universities and Colleges of Canada (AUCC) Awards Division

AUCC–Awards Division Programs

The AUCC–Awards Division administers fellowship and grant programs for Canadian citizens to study internationally. The programs are sponsored by other nations and are intended for Canadian graduate students concentrating in a variety of subject areas. Some previous locations for international study have included Ghana, Hong Kong, India, Jamaica, Nigeria, Sierra Leone, Sri Lanka, Trinidad and Tobago, Australia, New Zealand, and the United Kingdom.

qualifications: Canadian citizenship; enrollment in a graduate program at a Canadian institution

stipend: Tuition plus travel and living allowances

deadline: Varies by location of fellowship

contact: Association of Universities and Colleges of Canada Awards Division
Enquiries Clerk
151 Slater Street
Ottowa, Ontario KIP 5N1/Canada
(613) 563-1236

Belgian-American Education Foundation, Inc.

Graduate Exchange Fellowships

The Belgian-American Education Foundation funds exchange programs, fellowships, and research to promote closer relations between Belgium and the United States.

qualifications: U.S. or Belgian students and scholars

stipend: $10,000 to $22,500

deadline: December 31

contact: Dr. Emile L. Boulpaep
Belgian-American Education Foundation, Inc.
195 Church Street
New Haven, CT 06510/USA
(203) 777-5765

Robert Bosch Foundation

Robert Bosch Foundation Fellowship Program

The fellowships offer successful applicants an opportunity to work in the private and public sectors in Germany and to participate in three seminars, including a German-language seminar in Bonn, a "Deutschland" seminar in Berlin, and the Europe seminar in Paris and Brussels.

qualifications: U.S. citizenship and a graduate or professional degree or equivalent professional experience in business administration, economics, public affairs, political science, law, journalism, or mass communications. Knowledge of German highly recommended.

duration: Nine months to one academic year

stipend: DM 3,000 per month to cover food and lodging

deadline: October 15

contact: The Robert Bosch Foundation Fellowship Program
CDS International, Inc.
330 Seventh Avenue, Nineteenth Floor
New York, NY 10001/USA
(212) 760-1400

Brookings Institution

Research Fellowships in Foreign Policy Studies

Resident fellowships are awarded to doctoral candidates whose dissertation topics are related to public policy issues of interest to the institution. Brookings currently emphasizes security policy and international economic issues.

qualifications:	Applicants must be nominated by their graduate departments; Brookings then communicates directly with the applicant. Participation of women and minorities is encouraged.
duration:	Twelve months
stipend:	$13,000
deadline:	Mid-February
nominations:	September through mid-December
contact:	Dr. Janne E. Nolan The Brookings Institution 1775 Massachusetts Avenue, NW Washington, DC 20036-2188/USA (202) 797-6000

Mary Ingraham Bunting Institute of Radcliffe College

Peace Fellowship

One fellowship is awarded to a woman working in domestic or international policy, or in conflict resolution among groups or nations. Involvement with peace issues may be of an activist or scholarly nature.

duration: September 1 to August 31
stipend: $25,000
deadline: January 15
contact: Peace Fellowship
The Bunting Institute of Radcliffe College
Fellowships Office
34 Concord Avenue
Cambridge, MA 02138/USA
(617) 495-8212

Business and Professional Women's Foundation

This organization works to improve women's economic status by promoting their employment at all levels in all occupations.

Grants/Fellowships

The foundation awards grants for doctoral research on women's economic issues and also provides scholarships to women seeking training and education to improve their job skills.

contact: Business and Professional Women's Foundation
2012 Massachusetts Avenue, NW
Washington, DC 20036/USA
(202) 293-1200

Canadian Studies Grant Programs

For more information about the fellowship opportunities offered by the government of Canada, contact the address below.

contact: Academic Relations Office
Canadian Embassy
501 Pennsylvania Avenue, NW
Washington, DC 20001/USA
(202) 682-1740

Canadian Studies Graduate Student Fellowship Program

This program promotes research in the social sciences, journalism, business, environment, humanities, law, and fine arts, with a view to contributing to a better knowledge and understanding of Canada or its relationship with the United States and other countries of the world. The purpose of the fellowship is to offer graduate students an opportunity to conduct part of their doctoral research in Canada.

qualifications: U.S. citizenship or permanent residency; enrollment as a full-time doctoral student at an accredited four-year U.S. or Canadian college or university; and completion of all doctoral requirements except the dissertation upon application. Dissertations must be related in substantial part to the study of Canada.

duration: Up to nine months

stipend: Maximum of U.S.$850 per month

deadline: October 30

contact: See address above

Canadian Studies Faculty Enrichment Program

The Faculty Enrichment (Course Development) Program provides faculty with an opportunity to develop courses that will be offered as part of their regular teaching load. Courses in social sciences, journalism, business, environment, humanities, law, and fine arts with a unique relevance to Canada or the bilateral or North American relationship are eligible for consideration.

qualifications: Full-time faculty membership at an accredited four-year U.S. college or university. Applicants must have held a full-time teaching position for at least two years at their present institution and should be able to demonstrate that they are already teaching or will be authorized to teach courses with substantial Canadian content (33 percent or more). Team-teaching applications welcome.

duration: Up to three months

stipend: U.S.$1,500 per month

deadline: October 30

contact: See address above

Canadian Studies Faculty Research Grant Program

The purpose of the grant is to assist scholars in writing an article-length manuscript of publishable quality and reporting their findings in scholarly publications, with a view to contributing to the development of Canadian studies in the United States.

qualifications: Full-time faculty membership at an accredited four-year U.S. college or university or position at a U.S. research and policy-planning institute that involves significant Canadian, Canadian–U.S., or Canadian–North American research projects

stipend: U.S.$1,000 to $7,500

deadline: September 30

contact: See address above

Canadian Studies Sabbatical Fellowship Program

This grant is awarded to assist scholars who are on their first sabbatical leave devoted to a project on Canada. It is intended to fund the writing of a manuscript and its publication reporting in a scholarly journal.

qualifications:	Full-time faculty membership at an accredited four-year U.S. college or university; on a first sabbatical leave undertaking significant Canadian, Canadian-U.S. or Canadian–North American research projects
stipend:	U.S.$8,000 to $12,000
deadline:	September 30
contact:	See address above

Canadian Studies Senior Fellowship Award

The Senior Fellowship Award provides senior scholars with an opportunity to complete and publish a major study that will significantly benefit the development of Canadian studies in the United States. A limited number of fellowships are awarded, and only to academics with a lengthy track record in teaching, researching, and publishing on Canada or the bilateral or North American relationship. Preference in such instances is to fund a book project after a publisher has indicated an interest. This award is available only once to the same recipient.

qualifications:	Full-time tenured faculty membership at an accredited four-year U.S. college or university; full involvement in Canadian studies. Canadianists should be in the process of completing research for a book or major monograph on a subject of widespread interest to the Canadian studies community in the United States as well as in Canada. Applicants are expected to be granted a leave of absence or sabbatical during the award period.
duration:	Up to six months
stipend:	Up to U.S.$3,000 per month
deadline:	October 30
contact:	See address above

Center for European Studies, Harvard University

James Bryant Conant Fellowships for Postdoctoral Research

Up to two postdoctoral fellowships are awarded for residential research, leading to publication, at the Center for European Studies. Some research-related travel is allowed.

qualifications:	U.S. or Canadian citizenship; intention to teach in North America and completion of dissertation within the five years prior to application
duration:	Twelve months
stipend:	Up to $32,000
deadline:	March 1
contact:	Program for the Study of Germany and Europe Center for European Studies Harvard University 27 Kirkland Street Cambridge, MA 02138/USA (617) 495-4303

Center for International Affairs (CFIA), Harvard University

The CFIA, a major research institution within the Faculty of Arts and Sciences at Harvard University, houses scholars and practitioners of international affairs doing independent research on current issues in international relations. It sponsors numerous seminars and academic workshops on a broad variety of topics in international relations and supports the publication of scholarly works by resident researchers. For more information about the CFIA and its programs, contact one of the individuals specified below or the following address.

contact: Center for International Affairs
Harvard University
1737 Cambridge Street
Cambridge, MA 02138/USA
(617) 495-4420
FAX: (617) 495-8292

Pre- and Postdoctoral Fellowships

Fellowships are awarded to support the work of young scholars in residence who are conducting research related to the CFIA'S current research programs. Previous years' programs have focused on topics such as international institutions in the post–Cold War context, international environmental institutions and compliance policies, and international security. CFIA research is likely to continue in any of these areas and in issues of ethnicity and nationalism. Scholars must conduct research in residence at CFIA.

qualifications: Completion of all course work and general examinations by the beginning of the year for which support is sought
stipend: Varies according to fellowship type
deadline: January or February
contact: See address above

Academy for International and Area Studies Scholars Program

The Harvard Academy for International and Area Studies established its Scholars Program to provide opportunities for advanced work at Harvard to individuals who show promise of becoming leading scholars at major universities. The program intends to assist those who are pursuing an academic career involving both a social science discipline and a particular area of the world. Having developed significant expertise in a given geographical area, the academy scholar gains further training in an established discipline or, having gained a high level of competence in a discipline, acquires further mastery of a given geographical area.

qualifications:	Doctoral candidates (Ph.D. or comparable professional school degree) and recent recipients of these degrees who may already hold teaching or research positions. Those who are still candidates for advanced degrees must complete all course work and general examinations by the beginning of the academic year for which they seek support.
stipend:	Predoctoral fellows: $20,000–$25,000; postdoctoral scholars: $30,000–$35,000; health insurance
deadline:	October 15
contact:	Christopher Briggs-Hale, Fellowship Coordinator The Harvard Academy for International and Area Studies Center for International Affairs 1737 Cambridge Street Cambridge, MA 02138/USA (617) 495-2137

John M. Olin Fellowships in National Security/ Economics and National Security

Fellowships are awarded to support young scholars conducting basic research in the broad area of security and strategic affairs, including the economics of these issues. Subjects of interest include the causes and conduct of war, military strategy and history, defense policy and institutions, economic security, defense economics, and the defense industrial base. Fellowships are solely for research conducted while in residence at the CFIA.

qualifications: Completion of all course work and general examinations by the beginning of the year for which support is sought

stipend: Predoctoral fellows: up to $16,500 plus university facilities fees and health insurance; postdoctoral fellows: up to $28,000 plus health insurance

deadline: February 1

contact: Amy Englehardt
John M. Olin Fellowship Program
Center for International Affairs
1737 Cambridge Street
Cambridge, MA 02138/USA
(617) 496-5495

Pre- and Postdoctoral Fellowships and Visiting Scholar Affiliations

The Program on Nonviolent Sanctions sponsors fellowships to support research on how and the degree to which nonviolent direct action provides an alternative to violence in resolving the problems of totalitarian rule, war, genocide, and oppression. Projects include the development of history and data collection protocols, comparative and case study analyses.

qualifications: Contact the program director to discuss research projects before officially applying

deadline: January

contact: Program on Nonviolent Sanctions
Center for International Affairs
1737 Cambridge Street
Cambridge, MA 02138/USA
(617) 495-5580

Advanced Research Fellowships

The Program on U.S.-Japan Relations sponsors fellowships to support the work of scholars engaged in the study of contemporary Japan and U.S.-Japan relations. Subjects of interest include issues or problems in contemporary U.S.-Japan relations, Japan's international relations, and other studies that contribute to the understanding of Japan's international behavior.

qualifications: Postdoctoral scholars; preference is given to scholars from the United States, but others, especially from Pacific Rim countries, may apply

stipend: $26,000

deadline: March

contact: Program on U.S.-Japan Relations
Center for International Affairs
1737 Cambridge Street
Cambridge, MA 02138/USA
(617) 495-1890

Center for International Security and Arms Control, Stanford University

Center for International Security and Arms Control Fellowships

The purpose of the program is to contribute to training in the fields of international security, defense planning, and arms control.

qualifications: Advanced predoctoral students and postdoctoral scholars. Women and minorities are encouraged to apply.

duration: Twelve months

stipend: Determined on a case-by-case basis, with an average of $45,000; health insurance; funds for travel and other research-related expenses

contact: Director of Fellowship Programs
Center for International Security
   and Arms Control
320 Galvez Street
Stanford, CA 94305/USA
(415) 723-9626
FAX: (415) 723-0089

Center for International Studies, University of Missouri–St. Louis

Theodore Lentz Postdoctoral Fellowship in Global Issues, International Conflict and Peace

One postdoctoral fellowship is offered to support research in the area of global issues, international conflict, and peace studies. The fellow also teaches one introductory peace studies course in the fall semester and develops a second course to be taught in the spring.

qualifications:	Ph.D. degree from a university program in peace studies, international relations, or the equivalent
duration:	One year
stipend:	$21,000 salary for the year plus travel and expense allowance
deadline:	Selection process begins May 1; applications accepted until the position is filled
contact:	Dr. Joel Glassman Director, Center for International Studies University of Missouri–St. Louis 8001 Natural Bridge Road St. Louis, MO 63121-4499/USA (314) 553-5755

Center for Latin American Studies, University of Pittsburgh

Foreign Language and Area Studies Fellowships

Fellowships are awarded to advance students' knowledge of the languages and cultures of Latin America. Selection of fellows is based on academic record, letters of recommendation, intent of study plan, and priorities of the United States Department of Education, which gives final approval.

qualifications: U.S. citizenship or permanent residency in the United States; full-time enrollment in an advanced degree program as well as in a graduate certificate program of Latin American studies. Application must be submitted by the dean/chairperson of the school/department in which the student will study.

duration: Fall and spring terms; renewable

stipend: $8,000 stipend plus tuition and fee coverage for two terms

deadline: February 15

contact: Assistant Director
Center for Latin American Studies
University of Pittsburgh
4E31 Forbes Quadrangle
Pittsburgh, PA 15260/USA
(412) 648-7396

Center for U.S.-Mexican Studies, University of California, San Diego

Visiting Research Fellowships

Pre- and postdoctoral fellowships are awarded for research on North American economic integration; Mexican migration to the United States; environmental problems in Mexico and the U.S.-Mexico borderlands; and social, political, and economic change in Mexico.

qualifications:	U.S. citizenship; doctoral candidates or postdoctoral scholars and professionals
duration:	Three to ten months of continuous residence at the center
stipend:	Predoctoral scholars: $1,900 per month; postdoctoral scholars and senior professionals: monthly salary based on regular salary
deadline:	January 1
contact:	Graciela Platero, Fellowship Coordinator Center for U.S.-Mexican Studies University of California–San Diego La Jolla, CA 92093-0510/USA (619) 534-4503

Center on East-West Trade, Investment, and Communication, Duke University

Visiting Scholars Program

The East-West Center seeks to foster research on the political, social, cultural, and economic reforms that accompany the reintegration of the post-Communist world of the former Soviet Union into the international economy. The center's fellowship program, funded by the John D. and Catherine T. MacArthur Foundation, is intended to create a network of scholars producing written work on the issues crucial to Western understanding of post-Soviet societies, economies, and politics. These awards are not meant for scholars working on questions of arms control or general foreign policy questions.

qualifications: Young postdoctoral scholars working on book-length manuscripts or doctoral students in the advanced stages of their dissertations who plan to finish within one year. Applicants must be researching in the areas mentioned above; special consideration is given to proposals that focus on national, ethnic, and majority/minority questions.

duration: Eight months

stipend: Predoctoral scholars: up to $14,500; postdoctoral scholars: up to $22,500

deadline: Mid-March; awards announced in mid-April

contact: Center on East-West Trade, Investment, and Communications
Box 90401
Duke University
Durham, NC 27708-0401/USA
(919) 684-5551
FAX: (919) 684-8749

Centre for Transatlantic Foreign and Security Policy, Free University of Berlin

The Centre for Transatlantic Foreign and Security Policy solicits applications for research on security and international relations. Sponsored by the Volkswagen Foundation, the contest aims to help qualified young researchers in writing doctoral dissertations to prepare specifically for careers in policy advising, civil service (e.g., foreign affairs), the free market, or higher education. Priority is given to research that reviews politics theoretically and focuses on previously neglected issues. Possible topics include European and Atlantic cooperation; regional security and regionalism; theories of international relations in the context of security-related changes in the international system; problems in economic, technological, and ecological security; disarmament and arms control; human rights; the rights of minorities; intervention; and peacekeeping troops.

qualifications: Doctoral candidates at the dissertation level who are fluent in English and are willing to reside in Berlin for the course of the fellowship. Applicants should be no more than twenty-eight years old. Qualified women are expressly encouraged to apply.

contact: Prof. Dr. Helga Haftendorn
Arbeitsstelle Transatlantische Aussen- und Sicherheitspolitik
Freie Universität Berlin, FB Politische Wissenschaft
Ihnestrasse 21
14195 Berlin/Germany
(49-0-30) 838-4371 or 838-6671
FAX: (49-0-30) 838-6347

China Times Cultural Foundation

Scholarships

Scholarships are awarded to support undergraduate, graduate, and Chinese-language studies. Emphasis is on promoting Chinese culture, improvement in Chinese communities throughout the world, Sino-American cultural exchanges, Chinese-language education, scholarly discourse relating to Chinese studies, and other similar cultural and educational projects. Funding is primarily within the United States and China.

deadline: July 1

contact: James N. Tu
China Times Cultural Foundation
43-27 Thirty-sixth Street
Long Island City, NY 11101/USA
(718) 937-6110

Government of Colombia

Colombian Government Study and Research Grants

In conjunction with the Colombian Institute for Educational Loans and Advanced Studies Abroad (ICETEX), the study aid agency, and administered by the Institute of International Education, the Colombian government sponsors study and research grants for graduate work. Candidates in most fields are considered, but preference is given to applicants in agriculture, biology, business administration, chemistry, economics, education, engineering, geography, health services administration, history, Latin American literature, law, linguistics, physics, political science, public health, and regional development.

qualifications: U.S. citizenship and a college degree. Preference is given to mature candidates with experience in teaching and research.

duration: Up to two years of graduate work

deadline: October 31

contact: U.S. Student Program Division
Institute of International Education
809 United Nations Plaza
New York, NY 10017/USA
(212) 984-5330

Commission of the European Community

See European Community

Committee on Scholarly Communications with China

Contact the address below for more information about the committee's programs.

contact:	Committee on Scholarly Communications with China 1055 Thomas Jefferson Street, NW, Suite 2013 Washington, DC 20007/USA (202) 332-1250

Research Program

The committee supports in-depth, postdoctoral research on China, the Chinese portion of a comparative study, or exploratory research on an aspect of contemporary China. Funding supports limited research in Hong Kong or elsewhere in East Asia to supplement research within the People's Republic of China.

qualifications:	U.S. citizenship; Ph.D. Research must be within the social sciences or humanities.
deadline:	Mid-October
contact:	See address above

Graduate Program

This committee program supports graduate students enrolled in U.S. institutions who want to do course work toward their doctorates and/or research for their dissertations at a Chinese university or research institute.

qualifications:	M.A.; proficiency in Chinese equivalent to at least three years of college-level study
duration:	Minimum of one year
deadline:	Mid-October
contact:	See address above

China Conference Travel Grants

The commission sponsors grants to cover partial travel costs for U.S. scholars to report recent research findings at conferences in China. Grants do not support travel in order to lecture, teach or consult, or attend conferences dealing primarily with the improvement of teaching methods.

qualifications: U.S. citizenship or permanent residency; Ph.D. in the social sciences or humanities
stipend: Partial travel costs reimbursed after the conference upon receipt of report
deadline: Varies by the date of the conference
contact: See address above

Chinese Fellowships for Scholarly Development

These fellowships support Chinese scholars intending to do postdoctoral research at U.S. institutions. Scholars must be nominated by a U.S. host for residence at the host's institution for research and collaborative academic programs. The fellowships do not support Chinese scholars enrolled in degree programs. Preference is given to nominees whose hosts secure support for a second semester.

qualifications: Chinese citizenship; M.A. and Ph.D. or its equivalent from a Chinese institution
duration: One semester (five months)
stipend: Living and modest travel expenses
deadline: Mid-November
contact: See address above

Commonwealth Fund

The Harkness Fellowship Program

This program funds graduates of British, Australian, and New Zealand universities selected for American Political Science Association programs. See above for APSA listing.

qualifications: Recent graduate of British, Australian, or New Zealand universities

contact: The Harkness Fellowships
of the Commonwealth Fund
1 East Seventy-fifth Street
New York, NY 10021/USA
(212) 535-0400

Council for European Studies, Columbia University

Predissertation Fellowships

Fellowships allow graduate students in the beginning stages of their dissertation work the opportunity to pursue short-term exploratory research in western or southern Europe in order to define the scope of their proposed dissertations. This fellowship cannot be used jointly with another research fellowship in Europe.

qualifications: Graduate students whose dissertation proposals have *not* been approved

stipend: $3,000 for travel and living expenses

deadline: February 1

contact: Council for European Studies
Box 44, Schermerhorn Hall
Columbia University
New York, NY 10027/USA
(212) 854-4172

Council on Foreign Relations

International Affairs Fellowships

Fellowships are designed to give those in the academic and professional fields opportunities to engage in policy formation and to provide those from the policymaking sector with an opportunity to do research on substantive and process issues in foreign policy. Senior professionals may nominate; self-nominations are also acceptable.

qualifications: U.S. citizens between the ages of twenty-seven and thirty-five. Ph.D. or extensive experience in an academic or professional setting preferable.

duration: One year (short-term projects not eligible)

stipend: Within a fixed maximum, the council generally attempts to meet the major portion of a fellow's current income

deadline: Nomination deadline September 15; applications due October 31

contact: Director, International Affairs Fellowships Program
Council on Foreign Relations
58 East Sixty-eighth Street
New York, NY 10021/USA
(212) 734-0400

Frederick Douglass Institute for African and African-American Studies, University of Rochester

Postdoctoral Fellowship

Fellowships are offered to postdoctoral scholars researching historical and contemporary topics on the economy, society, politics, and culture of Africa and its diaspora. While completing their projects, fellows have departmental affiliation, teach one course, and conduct a seminar.

qualifications:	Postdoctoral scholars
duration:	One academic year
stipend:	$24,000
deadline:	January 31
contact:	Associate Director for Research and Curriculum Frederick Douglass Institute for African and African-American Studies University of Rochester 302 Morey Hall Rochester, NY 14627/USA (716) 275-7235

Earhart Foundation

Earhart Fellowship Research Grants

The program emphasizes the social sciences and the humanities; its objective is to foster the advancement of knowledge through teaching, lecturing, and publication. Applicants for the Earhart Fellowship must be nominated by a graduate professor, who is invited by the board of trustees to the annual meeting. No outside applications are accepted.

qualifications: Graduate student in the social sciences who has been nominated by a selected professor

deadline: None; 120 days required to process grant request

contact: Earhart Foundation
Plymouth Building, Suite 204
2929 Plymouth Road
Ann Arbor, MI 48105/USA
(313) 761-8592

East-West Center

Located in Hawaii, the East-West Center works to promote better relations and understanding among the nations of Asia, the Pacific, and the United States through cooperative study, training, and research. To this end, the East-West Center sponsors several fellowship and grant programs for research on issues relating to Asia and the Pacific. The center's programs are conducted in six problem-oriented institutes: communication and journalism, cultural studies, environment, international economics and politics, resources, and Pacific Island development. For information on the programs highlighted below, contact the following address.

contact: Award Services Officer
East-West Center
1777 East-West Road
Honolulu, HI 96848/USA
(808) 955-7735

East-West Center Fellows

Fellows are invited from research institutions, universities, government administrations, and business firms.

qualifications: U.S. citizen or permanent resident or Asian/Pacific Islander in the Exchange Visitor Program who has engaged in research and development activities on problems of interest to the center
duration: One week to three years
stipend: Monthly, relates to academic or professional status and rank
deadline: None
contact: See address above

East-West Center Jefferson Fellowships

Fellowships are available for U.S. midcareer and senior journalists and news broadcasters to work and study with their Asian/Pacific Islander counterparts in a ten-week program each spring. To increase knowledge of Asia among key desk editors and writers and to provide an opportunity for Asian/Pacific newspeople to learn more about the United States, five weeks of study at the East-West Center is followed by five weeks of travel in Asia for U.S. fellows and on the U.S. mainland for Asian/Pacific fellows.

qualifications: Qualified journalists from the United States and from the Asian/Pacific area, ranging from Japan to Iran, to Australia and New Zealand, including the Pacific Island nations

duration: Ten weeks

deadline: September 15

contact: See address above

East-West Center Graduate Degree Students Program

Highly promising graduate students are enabled to participate in research and development projects while studying for advanced degrees in a wide variety of disciplines at the University of Hawaii.

qualifications: U.S. citizen or permanent resident or Asian/Pacific Islander in the Exchange Visitor Program; must meet center guidelines and academic requirements for completing his or her degree

duration: Twelve to twenty-four months for those working on master's degrees; twelve to forty-eight months for those working toward doctoral degrees

deadline: December 1

contact: See address above

East-West Center Joint Predoctoral Research Fellowships

Doctoral students who have completed all course work may be awarded internships in which they gain supervised practical research experience in specific center projects. These awards require agreement among the center, the doctoral candidate, and the degree-granting institution.

qualifications:	Citizen or permanent resident of the United States or Asian/Pacific Islander in the Exchange Visitor Program; completion of all course requirements for the doctorate at an institution in the United States, Asia, or the Pacific
duration:	Six to twelve months
stipend:	$1,250 maximum monthly stipend
deadline:	January 15
contact:	See address above

East-West Center Postdoctoral Fellowships

The purpose of the fellowships is to provide support for revising the applicant's dissertation for book publication. Selection is based on the quality of the dissertation and its potential contribution to understanding about Asia and the Pacific, including culture and communication, population and demographic change, economic development and trade, energy and mineral resources, environmental management, and international relations, as well as other fields in the social sciences, humanities, and applied natural sciences.

qualifications:	U.S. citizen or permanent resident or one who meets the requirements of the Exchange Visitor Program (J-Visa); recent recipients of doctorates whose dissertations deal with contemporary issues in Asia and the Pacific
duration:	Up to twelve months
stipend:	$2,500 monthly stipend plus transportation to and from Honolulu and research expenses up to $1,000 for manuscript preparation
deadline:	January 15
contact:	See address above

East-West Center Professional Associates Awards

The awards are intended to attract leaders and mid- and upper-echelon managers of government, business, and education to specific East-West Center projects to apply research results to practice, develop, and demonstrate materials and test knowledge for policy. Activities include seminars, workshops, conferences, and planning meetings.

qualifications: Citizen or permanent resident of the United States or Asian/Pacific Islander in the Exchange Visitor Program; must be policymaker, public official, or manager in business, government, or education

duration: One to eight weeks

stipend: $30 a day

deadline: Varies according to project

contact: See address above

Friedrich Ebert Foundation

For information on the programs listed below, contact the following addresses:

Friedrich Ebert Foundation
1155 15th Street, NW, Suite 1100
Washington, DC 20005/USA
(202) 331-1819

Friedrich Ebert Foundation
950 Third Avenue,
    Twenty-eighth Floor
New York, NY 10022/USA
(212) 688-8770

German nationals interested in fellowships should contact FES Headquarters directly:

Friedrich-Ebert-Stiftung
Abt. Studienförderung
Godesberger Allee 149
53175 Bonn/Germany
(49-0-228) 883-0

Predissertation/Advanced Graduate Fellowships

The fellowships provide an opportunity for advanced graduate students to study and do research under the guidance of a university professor in Germany and to develop a dissertation proposal or to complete a specific research project.

qualifications:	U.S. citizenship; proficiency in German; student of political science, sociology, history, or economics
duration:	Five to twelve months
stipend:	DM 1,010 per month
deadline:	Due in Germany by February 28 for the next academic year
contact:	See address above

Doctoral Research Fellowships

Fellowships are available to allow doctoral candidates to spend time in Germany to conduct research necessary for their dissertations. Sociohistorical studies and studies in contemporary history and on current political problems (including comparative studies) are given special consideration.

qualifications:	Qualified Ph.D. students in political science, sociology, history, or economics at U.S. universities who have completed all course requirements for their doctorates and have an approved dissertation proposal; U.S. citizenship; proficiency in German
duration:	Five to twelve months
stipend:	DM 1,150 per month
deadline:	Due in Germany by February 28 for the next academic year
contact:	See address above

Postdoctoral/Young Scholar Fellowships

The program allows young scholars an opportunity to do independent research in Germany. Priority consideration is given to applicants who wish to carry out studies on politically relevant subjects, particularly those involving a comparative approach.

qualifications:	U.S. citizenship; proficiency in German; Ph.D. plus at least two years' experience in research and/or teaching at universities or in related research institutions within the disciplines of political science, sociology, history, and economics
duration:	Five to twelve months
stipend:	DM 1,490 per month
deadline:	Due in Germany by February 28 for the next academic year
contact:	See address above

Albert Einstein Institution

Fellows Program

Support is offered for a substantive research project promising a significant contribution to the study of nonviolent action.

qualifications: Doctoral candidates undertaking dissertation research or writing dissertations; advanced scholars undertaking specific research projects; and practitioners in past or present nonviolent struggles preparing documentation, description, and analysis of conflicts

duration: Twelve months; renewals considered

deadline: January 1

contact: Ronald M. McCarthy, Director
Einstein Institution
1430 Massachusetts Avenue
Cambridge, MA 02138/USA
(617) 876-0311

Eisenhower Exchange Fellowships

The fellowships are designed to send U.S. citizens to other countries or regions to promote exchange of ideas and international understanding. The program focuses on a series of professional visits and appointments with experts and includes cultural sites and hospitality by citizens of the host country. The fellow's spouse is invited and encouraged to participate.

qualifications: U.S. citizens between the ages of twenty-eight and forty-five with an advanced academic degree or significant experience in the private, government, or independent sectors

duration: Four weeks

stipend: Travel and expenses

deadline: Varies by program

contact: Eisenhower Exchange Fellowships
256 South Sixteenth Street
Philadelphia, PA 19102/USA
(215) 546-1738

European Community (EC)

Directorate-General Information, Communication, Culture Programs

Grants for research are awarded to young university teachers, assistants, and junior lecturers at the start of their careers who are doing research on European integration either individually or as a team. Award holders must present their work in one of the official EC languages.

qualifications: Young leaders from outside the EC with some professional interest in the EC

duration: One year

deadline: March 31

contact: Directorate-General Information
Commission of the European Communities
200, rue de la Loi
1049 Bruxelles/Belgium

In the United States, contact one of the Press and Information Offices of Delegations of the European Community, for example:

Delegation of the Commission of the European Communities
2100 M Street, NW, Seventh Floor
Washington, DC 20037/USA
(202) 862-9500
FAX: (202) 429-1766

The European Community's Visitors Programme

The EC Visitors Programme (ECVP) invites young leaders from countries outside the EC to visit Europe to gain a firsthand appreciation of the EC's goals, policies, and peoples and to increase mutual understanding between professionals from non-EC countries and their EC counterparts. An ECVP visit consists of an individually tailored program of meetings with officials at the EC institutions in Brussels, Luxembourg, and Strasbourg. In addition, participants may visit one other EC country. Twenty-four visitors from the United States are selected each year; 125 are selected worldwide.

qualifications:	Government officials (local, state, and federal); journalists; trade unionists; academics; officials of nonprofit, nongovernmental organizations; and other professionals in their mid-twenties to mid-forties with career-related interests in the EC. Participants must have completed a university education or equivalent training and have been employed for several years in their chosen career field. Not open to students.
duration:	Two weeks
stipend:	Travel and per diem costs
deadline:	March 1, for the following year
contact:	U.S. citizens should send applications to: Mr. Peter Doyle, Director Press and Public Affairs, Attn: ECVP Delegation of the Commission of the European Communities 2100 M Street, NW, Seventh Floor Washington, DC 20037/USA (202) 862-9500 FAX: (202) 429-1766 Other nationals should contact the Delegation of the Commission of the European Communities in their own countries for additional information.

ERASMUS Bureau Programs

The ERASMUS (European Community Action Scheme for the Mobility of University Students) Bureau sponsors scholarship programs to increase the mobility of university students and the development of international university cooperation in the EC. Financial support is available for interuniversity cooperation programs involving student and staff exchanges, joint curriculum development, and intensive programs. All fields of study are acceptable; programs are tenable at any higher education institution in an EC member state.

contact:	ERASMUS Bureau 15, rue d'Arlon 1040 Bruxelles/Belgium

European Development Fund

Scholarships are available to citizens of African, Caribbean, and Pacific countries associated with the EC to fund participation in courses related to EC development projects. Courses can be located in any of the EC member states.

qualifications: Citizenship in African, Caribbean, or Pacific country associated with the EC

stipend: Course fees, books, and field trips; international travel expenses; insurance; monthly allowance; stipend

contact: Information and application forms can be obtained from the EC diplomatic representative in the candidate's own country. The application is submitted through the candidate's employer and government.

EC-ASEAN Fellowship Programme

Fellowships are awarded to citizens of Indonesia, Malaysia, Singapore, Brunei, Thailand, and the Philippines for study in the EC member states.

qualifications: Citizenship in Indonesia, Malaysia, Singapore, Brunei, Thailand, or the Philippines

stipend: Course fees, books, and field trips; international travel expenses; insurance; monthly allowance; and a stipend to cover initial relocation expenses

contact: Information can be obtained from the British Council in the candidate's own country

European Community Studies Association (ECSA)

ECSA Dissertation Fellowships

Fellowships are offered to doctoral candidates who are preparing dissertations on the EC.

qualifications:	U.S. citizens enrolled in Ph.D. programs who have fulfilled all requirements prior to the doctoral dissertation. Applicants should be student members of ECSA or affiliated with universities that are institutional members.
stipend:	Up to $2,500 for travel in connection with research, books, documents and supplies, manuscript preparation, or other activities associated with the completion of the doctoral dissertation
contact:	ECSA Dissertation Fellowship Committee c/o Chair, Institute of International Studies University of South Carolina Columbia, SC 29208/USA (803) 777-8180

European Free Trade Association (EFTA)

Postgraduate Scholarships

Scholarships are awarded to support the early stages of postgraduate research into the role of EFTA in the EC.

qualifications:	Postgraduate research must be conducted in English, Finnish, French, German, Icelandic, Italian, Norwegian, or Swedish
deadline:	February 15
contact:	Press and Information Service 9-11, rue de Varembe 1211 Geneva 20/Switzerland (41-22) 34-90-00 FAX: (41-22) 33-92-91

European University

Scholarships

Scholarships are awarded for study at the European University in Versailles, France.

qualifications:	Student at the undergraduate level
duration:	Up to four years
stipend:	Up to 50 percent of tuition costs
contact:	F. X. Jean, Assistant Dean European University 35, rue des Chantiers 78000 Versailles/France (33-1) 30-21-11-77

European University Institute

Jean Monnet Fellowship

Fellowships are awarded to support postdoctoral research on modern and contemporary European history, EC law, law of West European countries, sociology, political science, and economics at the European University Institute in Florence, Italy.

qualifications:	Postdoctoral scholars
duration:	One year
stipend:	Travel, living expenses, and dependents' expenses
deadline:	December 1
contact:	Advisor for Academic Affairs European University Institute C.P. No. 2330, Firenze Ferrovia 50100 Florence/Italy (39-55) 50-92-32-1

Fondation Franco-Américaine

Fondation Franco-Américaine Fellowships

In conjunction with the American Political Science Association, the foundation provides fellowships for French professionals working in the public sector.

qualifications: French citizenship; fluency in English and experience in the public sector

contact: Fondation Franco-Américaine
38, avenue Hoche
75008 Paris/France

Ford Foundation

Ford Foundation International Affairs Grants

The premise of this program is that there is a continuing need for specialists in independent institutions that can provide authoritative analyses of important international issues for both policymakers and the public at large. To help meet this need, grants are made in the United States and abroad for research, training, the development of networks of analysts, and public information on seven topics: international economics and development; peace, security, and arms control; international refugees and migration; U.S. foreign policy; international relations, particularly in developing countries; international organizations and law; and foreign-area studies primarily relating to the former Soviet Union and Eastern Europe.

deadline: Applications accepted at any time

contact: Vice President, Program Division
Ford Foundation
320 East Forty-third Street
New York, NY 10017/USA
(212) 573-5000

Ford Foundation–funded programs are listed under the National Academy of Sciences and the School of Public Affairs at the University of Maryland. See specific listings for more information.

Foundation for Education and Research in International Studies (FERIS)

Albert Gallatin Fellowship in International Affairs

The foundation awards fellowships for study at the Graduate Institute of International Studies at the University of Geneva, Switzerland, which provides doctoral instruction in international law and politics, international economics, international institutions, and international development. French and English are used in all aspects of the institute's program.

qualifications: Doctoral candidates actively engaged in dissertation research within the field of international relations

duration: One academic year

stipend: SFr 1,700 a month for living expenses; airfare from New York to Geneva

deadline: Mid-March

contact: Allen Lynch
FERIS Foundation of America
34 Oak Ridge Road
Mount Kisco, NY 10549/USA
(914) 666-5720

Government of France

The French government sponsors several scholarships for study in France. Contact the French embassy in Washington, D.C., or the French Cultural Service in New York for more information.

contact: Embassy of France
Service du Conseiller Cultural
4101 Reservoir Road, NW
Washington, DC 20007-2178/USA
(202) 944-6000

Bourses Chateaubriand (Humanities)

Chateaubriand Scholarships are offered to doctoral students and postdoctoral scholars who would benefit from association with a French research institute or the use of French archives. Research should pertain to economics, history, archaeology, law, political science, philosophy, psychology, sociology, literature, or linguistics.

qualifications: U.S. citizenship; sufficient proficiency in written and spoken French to be able to carry out the proposed research
duration: Ten months
stipend: Monthly installments of about Fr 9,000; health insurance; round-trip airfare
deadline: February 1
contact: Services Culturels Français
Service Universitaire–Bourses Chateaubriand
972 Fifth Avenue
New York, NY 10021-0144/USA
(212) 439-1400

Fulbright Scholar Program

See United States Information Agency

German Academic Exchange Service (DAAD)

Study Visit Research Grants for Faculty

The grants provide opportunities for scholars to pursue research at universities and other institutions in Germany.

qualifications:	Two years' teaching and/or research experience, Ph.D. or equivalent degree, and a research record in the proposed field
duration:	One to three months
stipend:	Monthly maintenance allowance
deadline:	November 1
contact:	German Academic Exchange Service (DAAD) 950 Third Avenue, Nineteenth Floor New York, NY 10022/USA (212) 758-3223 DAAD Ref. 315 Kennedyallee 50 53175 Bonn/Germany

Research Grants for Recent Ph.D.'s and Ph.D. Candidates

The grants support dissertation or postdoctoral research at libraries, archives, institutes, or laboratories in Germany.

qualifications:	Recent Ph.D. recipients (up to two years after the degree) not older than thirty-five and Ph.D. candidates not older than thirty-two
duration:	Two to six months
stipend:	Monthly allowance; international travel subsidy; health insurance
deadline:	November 1
contact:	See address above

DAAD-AICGS Summer Grant

See American Institute for Contemporary German Studies

DAAD sponsors many different programs ranging from language to law. Inquiries should be made to the address listed above.

German Historical Institute (DHI)

German Historical Institute Scholarship

This scholarship is for doctoral students working on topics related to the institute's general scope of interest; contact the DHI for specific information about this scope. U.S. applicants for these scholarships should be working on topics of German history for which they need to evaluate source material located in the United States.

qualifications:	Doctoral students
duration:	Three months to one year, with an average of six months
deadline:	Late May
contact:	German Historical Institute 1607 New Hampshire Avenue, NW Washington, DC 20009/USA (202) 387-3555

AICGS/DHI Fellowships in Postwar German History

See American Institute for Contemporary German Studies

The German Marshall Fund of the United States

Research Fellowships

Grants are offered to support research that will improve the understanding of significant contemporary economic, political, and social developments involving the United States and Europe. Both international and comparative domestic issues are eligible topics. The fund hopes to assist scholars at all stages of their careers.

qualifications: Completion of all degree requirements prior to filing the application and completion of at least one additional research project that has received critical review. Senior scholars must provide distinguished records of past research experience.

duration: One academic term to one year

stipend: Maximum amount $30,000

deadline: Mid-November

contact: The German Marshall Fund of the United States
11 Dupont Circle, NW
Washington, DC 20036/USA
(202) 745-3950

Graduate Fellowships for Global Change Program, Oak Ridge Associated Universities

Research Fellowships

This program provides one-year fellowships that can be renewed annually. Studies must focus on how to advance the science of global change.

qualifications: Must be in the early stages of graduate education

contact: Graduate Studies for Global Change Program
Science/Engineering Education Division
Oak Ridge Associated Universities
P.O. Box 117
Oak Ridge, TN 37831-0117/USA
(615) 576-7393

Government of Great Britain

British Marshall Scholarships

The British government annually offers scholarships for study leading to a degree at a British university.

qualifications: U.S. citizens who will be under twenty-six years of age on October 1 in the year in which the award is granted. At the time of taking up residence in a British university, applicants must have obtained a first degree, requiring at least three years' study, from a degree-granting university or college in the United States recognized by the appropriate accrediting association. A minimum qualification of a grade point average of 3.7 (or A– for academic courses after the freshman year) is normally required.

duration: Twenty-two months (two academic years); in certain circumstances may be extended for a third year

stipend: Tuition, residence, and related costs; may be a marriage allowance

applications available: June 1

deadline: Mid-October

contact: British Information Services
805 Third Avenue
New York, NY 10022/USA
(212) 745-0200
FAX: (212) 758-5395

Harry Frank Guggenheim Foundation

Harry Frank Guggenheim Foundation Grants

Funding is offered for research in the natural and social sciences and the humanities that will increase understanding of the causes, manifestations, and control of violence. Topics of interest to the foundation concern violence, aggression, and dominance in relation to social change; the socialization of children; intergroup conflict; drug trafficking and use; family relationships; and investigations of the control of aggression and violence. Priority is given to areas not receiving adequate exposure.

qualifications:	Doctoral students (grants to support the writing of dissertations) and postdoctoral scholars
duration:	One to two years
stipend:	$15,000 to $35,000
contact:	Harry Frank Guggenheim Foundation 527 Madison Avenue New York, NY 10022/USA (212) 644-4907

The Hague Academy of International Law

Scholarships for Sessions of Courses

Scholarships are awarded to aid summer study in the fields of private international law and public international law at The Hague Academy of International Law in the Netherlands. Some lectures are simultaneously interpreted into English.

qualifications:	Three years of law school or equivalent international experience
duration:	Summer session
deadline:	March 1
contact:	Secretariat Carnegieplein 2 Peace Palace 2517 KJ The Hague/Netherlands (31-70) 46 96 80

Harriman Institute for Advanced Study of the Soviet Union, Columbia University

Postdoctoral Fellowships

Fellowships are awarded to postdoctoral scholars to be in residence at the institute while revising their dissertations for publication. Evidence of a dissertation's potential to make a significant contribution to Russian, Soviet, or post-Soviet studies is weighed foremost in the selection.

qualifications: Recent Ph.D. recipients who have successfully defended their dissertations prior to the commencement of the fellowship

duration: One semester to one academic year

deadline: Early January

contact: Judith L. Chase, Program Assistant
Harriman Institute, Columbia University
420 West 118th Street, Room 1213
New York, NY 10027/USA
(212) 854-4623

The Hebrew University of Jerusalem

The Harry S. Truman Research Institute for the Advancement of Peace

The institute conducts research on the growth, history, and political and social development of the non-Western world, with particular emphasis on the Middle East. Each year the institute supports several visiting fellows from Western and non-Western countries.

qualifications: Distinguished scholars and senior professors

deadline: November

contact: The Harry S. Truman Research Institute for the Advancement of Peace
The Alfred A. Davis Family Building
The Hebrew University of Jerusalem
Mount Scopus, Jerusalem 91905/Israel
(972-2) 88-23-00
FAX (972-2) 82-80-76

The Raoul Wallenberg Scholarships

The scholarship program is dedicated to the examination of the function and role of leadership in democracies. The objective is to provide an opportunity for a select group of young men and women to study in a graduate-level visiting student program at the Hebrew University of Jerusalem. Candidates of diverse religious, racial, and ethnic backgrounds are encouraged to apply.

qualifications: Bachelor's degree from a U.S. university

duration: July through June

stipend: Full tuition for the academic year, an intensive Hebrew-language study program, and a $1,000 subsidy toward a round-trip ticket to Israel from New York City

deadline: February 16

contact: Office of Academic Affairs
The Hebrew University of Jerusalem
11 East Sixty-ninth Street
New York, NY 10021/USA
(212) 472-2288
FAX: (212) 517-4548

Hoover Institution on War, Revolution, and Peace

National Fellowships

The Hoover Institution awards annual fellowships for post-doctoral research on historical and public policy issues involving the United States in such fields as economics, education, international relations, law, modern history, political science, and sociology. Fellows spend one year researching at the Hoover Institution at Stanford University.

qualifications: Doctoral degree from a U.S. or Canadian university. Preference is given for those junior scholar applicants whose proposals embody empirical studies.

duration: September through August

deadline: January 10

contact: Wendy S. Minkin
Program Coordinator
National Fellows Program
Hoover Institution on War, Revolution, and Peace
Stanford, CA 94305-6010/USA
(415) 723-1687

Alexander von Humboldt Foundation

The Alexander von Humboldt Foundation is a German organization sponsoring fellowships for both German and non-German scholars. The use of "Foreign Scholars" in the program titles below indicates that the program is not for German citizens but all other nationals are eligible to apply. For information, contact the following address.

contact: Alexander von Humboldt Foundation
1350 Connecticut Avenue, NW, #903
Washington, DC 20036/ USA
(202) 296-2990
FAX: (202) 833-8514

Alexander von Humboldt Foundation
Jean-Paul Strasse 12
53173 Bonn/ Germany
(49-0-228) 833-0

Humboldt Research Fellowships for Foreign Scholars

The postdoctoral fellowships allow scholars to carry out research at institutes in Germany and other European countries.

qualifications: Ph.D. or equivalent degree; under forty years of age; a good command of German

duration: Six to twelve months, although extensions of up to twenty-four months may be granted upon application

stipend: Monthly stipend from DM 3,000 to DM 3,800

deadline: None; selection committee meets in March, July, and November

contact: See address above

Humboldt Research Awards for Foreign Scholars–Humanities Award

The award winners are funded for research stays at German institutions.

qualifications: Must be nominated by an eminent German scholar, be full or associate professors, and have internationally recognized research records

duration: Four to twelve months

contact: See address above

Bundeskanzler Scholarships for Future American Leaders

This fellowship is awarded to young U.S. citizens to pursue a year in Germany in an academic or other public institution. The scholarship is intended to maintain and foster the close relationship between the United States and Germany by creating connections with the future leaders of the United States.

qualifications: U.S. citizens between the ages of twenty-four and thirty-two, with significant experience beyond the bachelor's degree (preferably outside academia)

duration: One year

stipend: Monthly stipend up to DM 5,500; travel expenses; a study tour; an introductory seminar; costs for language learning and a final meeting in Bonn, Germany

deadline: October 31

contact: See address above

Max Planck Research Awards for Foreign and German Scholars

Approximately twenty-five Max Planck Research Awards are presented annually to internationally acknowledged non-German and German scholars who intend to pursue long-term, project-oriented research. Awards cover short periods of research at partner institutes; travel to partner institutes, joint academic conferences, and workshops; as well as any necessary additional funds for purchase of material or payment of assistants.

qualifications: Scholars from all disciplines and nationalities must be nominated by heads of German universities or research establishments. Priority is given to scientific cooperation between German and non-European scholars. Internationally recognized research work and planned joint research with a non-German partner are important considerations.

stipend: Up to DM 200,000

duration: Maximum of three years

deadline: None

contact: See address above

Research Fellowships for German Scholars

Two hundred Feodor Lynen Research Fellowships are granted annually to highly qualified German scholars intending to carry out research projects of their own choice at institutes of former Humboldt guest researchers abroad.

qualifications:	Doctoral degree, extensive academic qualifications and publications, a formal invitation by a former Humboldt fellow or award winner, a specific research plan, and a good command of English or the language of the host country
duration:	One to three years
stipend:	Monthly stipend of DM 2,500 to DM 2,800 (joint financing by the Humboldt Foundation and the host institute is desired); relocation expenses, travel, partial material and health insurance costs, and assistance upon returning to Germany
deadline:	None; selection committee meets in March, June or July, and November
contact:	See address for German headquarters above

Transatlantic Cooperation Program for Humanities Scholars

Cooperative research projects between German and U.S. scholars in the humanities and social sciences can receive funding up to $50,000 from the German side as long as equivalent matching funds are provided by U.S. sources. Preference is given to projects that pursue interdisciplinary approaches. Funds can be spent on travel expenses, materials, workshops, printing costs, and research assistantships.

qualifications:	Criteria include the project's potential for strengthening transatlantic cooperation, the originality of the research project, and the academic qualifications of the applicant. Applications must contain a research plan, curriculum vitae, publication list, time and cost tables and reference contacts in Germany and the United States.
deadline:	December 15
contact:	See address above

IBM South Africa Projects Fund

Scholarship Program

Scholarships are awarded to support education, legal services, business, and black business interests in South Africa. Funding is provided primarily to institutions, although some funding is allotted for scholarship funds for black South Africans.

deadline:	None
contact:	IBM South Africa Projects Fund c/o IBM Corporation Old Orchard Road, Room 3c-45 Armonk, NY 10504-1709/USA

Institut Européen des Hautes Etudes Internationales

Bourse de l'Institut Européen des Hautes Etudes Internationales

Fellowships are awarded to postgraduate scholars to pursue a study and research program in communications and international relations at the Institut Européen in Nice, France.

qualifications:	Doctoral degree; between the ages of twenty-one and thirty-five; good knowledge of French
duration:	Nine months
deadline:	End of June
contact:	Administrative Director Institut Européen des Hautes Etudes Internationales Palais de Marbre 9, avenue de Fabron 06200 Nice/France (33-93) 86-39-12

Institute for Humane Studies (IHS), George Mason University

IHS Claude R. Lambe Fellowships

Fellowships are available to undergraduate and graduate students of all nations and backgrounds to support the study of the human sciences, humanities, or related professional fields. Students from the departments of history, jurisprudence, economics and political economy, moral and political philosophy, psychology, sociology, journalism, communications, and literature are eligible.

qualifications:	Graduate students; juniors and seniors in college pursuing studies in one of the areas listed above
duration:	One year
stipend:	Up to $17,500
deadline:	January 15
applications available:	November
contact:	Institute for Humane Studies Lambe Fellowship Secretary George Mason University 4400 University Drive Fairfax, VA 22030-4444/USA (703) 323-1055

Institute for the Study of World Politics

Dissertation Fellowship Competition

The institute awards approximately twenty-five fellowships annually to young scholars whose work will develop knowledge and understanding essential to the resolution of fundamental international issues. Applicants may be citizens of any country.

qualifications: Doctoral candidates who have completed all course work and are conducting dissertation research in political science, economics, international relations, and history (and, on occasion, other social science disciplines)

duration: Three to nine months

deadline: Mid-February; awards announced in mid-May

contact: Stephen Paschke, Associate Director
Institute for the Study of World Politics
1775 Massachusetts Avenue, NW
Washington, DC 20036/USA
(202) 797-0882

Institute of International Education (IIE)

The IIE runs several fellowship programs funded by other organizations, including the Fulbright programs. Information about Fulbright programs can be obtained by contacting the Fulbright program advisor at academic institutions, the U.S. Information Agency (see listing below), or the IIE in New York at the address listed below.

Edgar M. Bronfman Fellowships for Economics in Eastern Europe

The fellowships are for graduate students and young professionals to pursue graduate studies abroad in economics. Two awards are currently offered: one for study in Moscow, the other for study in Prague, though the location for the fulfillment of the fellowship may change annually. The fellowships are contingent on funding.

qualifications:	Graduate students under thirty years of age with a bachelor's degree in business, economics, or related studies; proficiency in the language of the host country
deadline:	Late October
contact:	U.S. Student Programs Institute of International Education 809 United Nations Plaza New York, NY 10017/USA (212) 883-8200

International Human Rights Internship Program

IIE sponsors fellowships for graduate students or recent graduates to work for one year in human rights organizations in the United States, Europe, Africa, and Latin America.

duration:	One year
stipend:	$6,000 to $16,000, depending on location
deadline:	August 31
contact:	Annette Kuroda Institute of International Education 1400 K Street, NW Washington, DC 20005/USA (202) 898-0600

Institutional Reform and the Informal Sector (IRIS), University of Maryland

IRIS Research Program

IRIS provides technical and organizational assistance to promote institutional reform, particularly in the economic sector, in the Third World and in countries undergoing the transition from communism. The IRIS Scholars Program is intended for researchers from institutions outside the Washington metropolitan area and is not limited to individuals from university settings. Proposals dealing with virtually any part of the world are considered.

duration:	Half semester, summer, or some other period
stipend:	$320 per day
deadline:	Applications received and reviewed in February and September
contact:	Institutional Reform and the Informal Sector Morrill Hall, University of Maryland College Park, MD 20742/USA (301) 405-3110

Inter-American Foundation (IAF)

The IAF offers fellowships to support both grassroots development practitioners and applied researchers from the Caribbean, Latin America, and the United States. Fellows examine the efforts of the rural and urban poor to improve their lives, their methods of organization and production, and policies and programs designed to alleviate poverty.

Field Research Program at Master's/Doctoral Level

This program supports field research in Latin America and the Caribbean on grassroots development topics by graduate students enrolled in U.S. universities.

qualifications: Master's level: Enrollment in a master's degree or equivalent level program at the time of the field research. This program also covers pre-dissertation field research; doctoral level: Completion of all course requirements for the doctoral degree

stipend: Master's fellows: $1,000 to $3,000; doctoral fellows: $3,000 to $7,000

deadline: December 1

contact: Robert J. Sogge, Fellowship Officer
IAF Fellowship Programs–Dept. 555
901 North Stuart Street, Tenth Floor
Arlington, VA 22203/USA
(703) 841-3864
FAX: (703) 841-0973

U.S. Graduate Study Program for Latin American and Caribbean Citizens

This program assists development practitioners and researchers from Latin America and the Caribbean to pursue graduate studies in the United States. Candidates must make their own arrangements for admission to a U.S. university and have demonstrated interest in the problems of poverty and development.

qualifications:	Latin American or Caribbean citizenship, with experience in developmental fields. Candidates must be nominated by their home institutions and are expected to return to them.
stipend:	$5,000 to $15,000
deadline:	Mid-February or early March
contact:	See address above

Dante B. Fascell Inter-American Fellowship Program

This program supports grassroots development by distinguished Latin American and Caribbean leaders.

qualifications:	Latin American citizenship, with leadership experience and potential
duration:	Twelve months, beginning August 31
stipend:	$50,000
deadline:	March 1
contact:	See address above

International Education Center (IEC)

Fellowship Program to the People's Republic of China and the Former Soviet Union

Fellowships are offered to help defray the expenses of an IEC study tour to the People's Republic of China or areas of the former Soviet Union (primarily Russia). The trips are intended for individuals interested in Chinese studies and/or Russian studies.

qualifications: U.S. or Canadian citizenship; no educational eligibility requirements

duration: Sixteen to twenty-two days

contact: Newsletter Editor
International Education Center
Bowling Green Station
Box 843
New York, NY 10274/USA
(212) 747-1755

International Federation of University Women (IFUW)

The IFUW Ida Smedley MacLean International Fellowships

The fellowships are awarded to encourage advanced scholarship and original research by enabling university women to undertake research in countries other than those in which they live or have received their educations.

qualifications: Applicants should be under fifty and must be well started on a research program; fellowships are not awarded for the first year of a Ph.D. program. If an applicant submits a publication in any language other than English or French, she should include a resume in either of these languages.

duration: At least eight months of work

stipend: SFr 8,000 to 10,000

deadline: Affiliate members: December 1; independent IFUW members: September 15

applications available: Members of IFUW interested in applying should contact their national federations or associations, who forward a limited number of applications to the Committee for the Award of International Fellowships. Other applicants should obtain forms from IFUW headquarters.

contact: International Federation of University Women
37, quai Wilson
1201 Geneva/Switzerland
(41-22) 731-23-80
FAX: (41-22) 738-04-40

The Winifred Cullis Grants

The Winifred Cullis Fund assists women graduates who are members of a national federation or association of university women affiliated to IFUW or independent members. Grants are given for carrying out independent research, obtaining specialized training essential to the applicant's research, and training in new techniques. Funding may be used for work in any academic discipline, preferably in a country other than that in which the candidate has received her education or habitually resides.

qualifications:	Applicants must have completed at least one year of graduate work and be well started on their research programs before applying for a grant. Grants are not usually awarded to candidates over fifty.
stipend:	SFr 3,000 to 6,000
deadline:	Affiliate members: December 1; independent IFUW members: September 15
applications available:	See instructions above
contact:	See address above

The Dorothy Leet Grants

The Dorothy Leet Fund assists women graduates of countries with a comparatively low per capita income who are members of a national federation or association affiliated with IFUW or who are independent members. Grants may also be given to other women graduates who wish eventually to work as experts in these countries or whose research is of value to such countries.

qualifications:	Applicants should be engaged in independent research or projects or have plans to obtain training essential to research or to new techniques related to group work. They should be of sufficient capacity and maturity to make a significant contribution to the needs of the country with which their work is concerned. Grants are not usually awarded to candidates over fifty.
stipend:	SFr 3,000 to 6,000
deadline:	Affiliate members: December 1; independent IFUW members: September 15
applications available:	See instructions above
contact:	See address above

International Research and Exchanges Board, Inc. (IREX)

IREX's basic purposes are to guarantee access by U.S. scholars to research resources in the former Soviet Union, Eastern Europe, and Mongolia and to encourage scholarly cooperation with the region in the humanities and social sciences. IREX's main office is in Washington, but there are offices in Albania, Bulgaria, the Czech Republic, Latvia, Hungary, Poland, Romania, and the former Yugoslavia, and Alma-Ata, Kiev, and Moscow in the former Soviet Union. Citizens of these countries should contact the IREX office in their home country for information. For information about all of these programs, contact the address below.

contact: International Research
and Exchanges Board, Inc.
1616 H Street, NW
Washington, DC 20006/USA
(202) 628-8188
FAX: (202) 628-8189

Individual Advanced Research Opportunities for U.S. Scholars in the States of the Former Soviet Union

Research opportunities are available in Armenia, Azerbaijan, Belarus, Estonia, Georgia, Kazakhstan, Kyrgyzstan, Latvia, Lithuania, Moldova, the Russian Federation, Tajikistan, Turkmenistan, Ukraine, and Uzbekistan to applicants in all disciplines. Awards are available to encourage long-term (nine to twelve months) research in the humanities and social sciences by postdoctoral scholars in geographic areas other than central Russia. Grants cover all expenses, regardless of sabbatical salaries or any other additional support.

qualifications: U.S. citizenship or permanent residency, command of the host-country language sufficient for research, and affiliation with a university as a faculty member or advanced doctoral candidate. Research residents must have a Ph.D. or equivalent professional degree; affiliation with a university is not required.

duration:	Two to twelve months
stipend:	25,000 for all expenses: round-trip transportation, visa fees, family allowance, housing, local travel
deadline:	November 1, for the next academic year
contact:	See address above

Individual Advanced Research Opportunities for U.S. Scholars in Central and Eastern Europe

IREX sponsors fellowships in all disciplines in Albania, Bulgaria, the Czech and Slovak Federal Republics, Hungary, Poland, Romania, and areas of the former Yugoslavia.

qualifications:	U.S. citizenship or permanent residency; strong command of the language of the proposed host country. Research applicants in modern foreign languages and area studies must apply simultaneously for Fulbright-Hays Grants through the U.S. Department of Education.
duration:	Two to twelve months
stipend:	Round-trip airfare, housing in the host country, a stipend in dollars plus funding for living expenses
deadline:	November 1, for the next academic year
contact:	See address above

Individual Advanced Research Opportunities for U.S. Scholars in Mongolia

Research opportunities are available for advanced predoctoral and postdoctoral scholars at institutions in Mongolia.

qualifications:	U.S. citizenship or permanent residency, command of Mongolian sufficient for research, and affiliation with a university as a faculty member or advanced doctoral candidate
duration:	Two to ten months
stipend:	Round-trip airfare and visa fees, housing, a research allowance, excess baggage allowance, and a stipend in dollars and tugriks
deadline:	November 1, for the next academic year
contact:	See address above

Developmental Fellowships

These fellowships are intended to prepare scholars for field research in the states of the former Soviet Union, Mongolia, or Central and Eastern Europe. Developmental Fellowships are limited to use in the United States; fellows are required to apply to an overseas IREX program following their tenures. Disciplinary projects, studies of Soviet nationalities, and studies to lead to dual-area competence are acceptable topics.

qualifications: Faculty members, postdoctoral researchers, or advanced Ph.D. candidates who will pursue research that will require study in the former Soviet Union, Central and Eastern Europe, or Mongolia. No support will be given for routine graduate course work or dissertation research.

duration: Three to twenty-four months

deadline: Mid-February

contact: See address above

Individual Advanced Research Opportunities in the United States for Scholars from the States of the Former Soviet Union

Long-term and short-term research placement and access to institutions in the United States are offered to predoctoral and postdoctoral scholars.

qualifications: Applicants must be citizens of Armenia, Azerbaijan, Belarus, Georgia, Kazakhstan, Kyrgyzstan, Moldova, Russian Federation, Tajikistan, Turkmenistan, Ukraine, or Uzbekistan and have a command of the English language sufficient for research. Applicants should also be affiliated with a university or research institution and have a candidate of sciences degree by commencement of the program.

duration: Three to twelve months

stipend: Housing, a stipend, insurance, travel arrangements to and from the research location, and international and domestic transportation

deadline: Mid-November, for the following March or September

contact: See address above or contact the IREX offices in Alma-Ata, Kiev, or Moscow

Individual Advanced Research Opportunities in the United States for Scholars from Central and Eastern Europe and the Baltics

Long-term research placement and access is offered to predoctoral and postdoctoral scholars. International transportation is provided in most cases by either IREX or the sending side.

qualifications:	Applicants must be citizens of Albania, Bosnia-Herzegovina, Bulgaria, Croatia, the Czech Republic, Estonia, Hungary, Latvia, Lithuania, Macedonia, Poland, Romania, the Slovak Republic, Slovenia, or the former Yugoslavia. Applicants must have a command of English sufficient for advanced academic research and normally must have an affiliation with a university or research institution as a faculty member or advanced doctoral candidate.
duration:	Three to twelve months
stipend:	Housing, a stipend, book and photocopy allowance, U.S. domestic travel, and medical insurance
deadline:	Varies within each country
contact:	See address above or contact the IREX offices in Tirana, Sofia, Prague, Riga, Budapest, Warsaw, Bucharest, or Belgrade

Individual Advanced Research Opportunities in the United States for Mongolian Scholars

Opportunities are provided for placement and access for advanced predoctoral and postdoctoral scholars at institutions in the United States.

qualifications: Mongolian citizenship, command of English sufficient for research, candidate of sciences degree, and affiliation with a university or research institution. Candidates are nominated by the Mongolian Academy of Sciences.

duration: Two to ten months

stipend: Round-trip transportation, housing, a dollar stipend, book allowance, health insurance, and language training

deadline: None

contact: Department of Foreign Relations
Mongolian Academy of Sciences
Sukhebaatar Square 3
Ulaanbaatar 11/ Mongolia

IREX sponsors several other fellowships for U.S. and other scholars. Contact the nearest IREX office for complete information.

Government of Japan

The government of Japan sponsors many specific scholarships and programs for study in Japan. For more information on these programs, contact one of the following organizations.

contact: Information Center
Association of
 International Education
4-5-29 Komaba,
 Meguro-ku,
Tokyo 153/Japan
(81-3) 485-6827
FAX: (81-3) 467-3834

Embassy of Japan
2520 Massachusetts
 Avenue, NW
Washington, DC
 20008/USA

or your local consulate general

Monbusho Scholarship (Research)

The Japanese Ministry of Education, Science, and Culture (Monbusho) sponsors a scholarship to enable students from 110 different countries to study in Japan. U.S. citizens may apply for several different programs, including programs for research at the graduate level at Japanese universities and educational institutions.

qualifications: Citizenship of the country in which recruitment occurs, under thirty-five years old, degree from a four-year college or university by one month prior to the fellowships; proficiency in Japanese and potential to receive instruction in Japanese

duration: Two to twelve months

stipend: Round-trip airfare to Japan, all school fees, an arrival allowance, and a monthly allowance of approximately 181,500 yen

deadline: Late August (varies; contact the nearest consulate for details)

contact: See address above

The Japan Foundation

The Japan Foundation Fellowship program provides scholars, researchers, and professionals with opportunities to do research in Japan in the humanities and social sciences.

Research Fellowship

These fellowships are intended for scholars, researchers, and professionals to do research in Japan.

qualifications:	Academic position in a research institution or equivalent analytical experience
duration:	Two to twelve months
stipend:	Monthly stipend up to 430,000 yen, with allowances for travel, settling in, and additional activities
deadline:	February 1
contact:	The Japan Foundation New York Office 152 West Fifty-seventh Street, Thirty-ninth Floor New York, NY 10019/USA (212) 489-0299

Doctoral Fellowship

This program provides doctoral candidates in the humanities and social sciences the opportunity to conduct research in Japan.

qualifications:	Completion of all academic requirements except the dissertation upon beginning of the fellowship; sufficient proficiency in Japanese
duration:	Four to fourteen months
stipend:	310,000 yen, with allowances for travel, settling in, and additional activities
deadline:	February 1
contact:	See address above

The Japan–United States Friendship Commission

The Japan–United States Friendship Commission is an independent federal agency dedicated to promoting mutual understanding and cooperation between the United States and Japan.

Japanese Studies

The Japanese studies program aims to increase U.S. scholars' understanding of Japan, most specifically in the professional fields of law, business, journalism, economics, and engineering. Most of the commission's funding goes directly to institutions, later to be disbursed among the researchers.

qualifications: U.S. citizenship. Applications should be filed through home academic institutions.

deadline: March 1 and August 1

contact: The Japan–United States Friendship Commission
1200 Pennsylvania Avenue, NW, Room 3416
Washington, DC 20004/USA
(202) 275-7712
FAX: (202) 275-7413

Policy-Oriented Research

The commission provides opportunities to those who seek to explain the fundamental issues of change in the structure of the economy, the nature of political leadership, Japan's international role, the dynamics of change in Japan's culture and society, and other contemporary issues. The commission expects researchers to convey their findings to the policymaking communities and to make the results widely available in the United States and Japan.

qualifications: Achievement in the field and willingness to work with the public policy communities to raise the quality of public debate between the two countries

deadline: March 1 and August 1

contact: See address above

American Studies

Opportunities are available for Japanese scholars to study major developments and changes in U.S. society.

qualifications: Japanese citizenship

deadline: March 1 and August 1

contact: See address above

Helen Kellogg Institute for International Studies, University of Notre Dame

Helen Kellogg Institute for International Studies Residential Fellowships

The institute seeks fellows of high scholarly accomplishment and promise, both at senior and junior levels, whose work and presence will contribute creatively to its major research themes. The institute's research reflects commitments to democracy, development, and social justice and focuses on five major themes: democratization and the consolidation of democracy; alternative paths to development; the role of religion and the Catholic church in Latin America; the public sector; and public policies for social justice.

qualifications: International candidates holding Ph.D.'s or equivalent degrees in any discipline of the social sciences or history. Candidates are evaluated individually but joint projects are considered. All non–U.S. fellows are requested to apply for travel grants to aid with transportation expenses in the United States.

deadline: November 15

contact: Academic Coordinator
Helen Kellogg Institute for International Studies
University of Notre Dame
0207 Hesburgh Center
Notre Dame, IN 46556/USA
(219) 239-6580

W. K. Kellogg Foundation

Kellogg International Study Grant

Long- and short-term grants are awarded to natives of Latin America, the Caribbean, or South Africa for study toward an advanced degree that can be used to improve the quality of life in recipients' home countries. Study grants are principally carried out in the United States. The long-term program is for twelve months of study in a non-degree-training program or to obtain a master's degree; twenty-four months are offered to obtain a doctoral degree. Short-term grants are for a maximum of six months and can be used for travel or academic purposes.

qualifications:	Latin American, Caribbean, or South African citizenship; bachelor's degree from a recognized university or professional school and acceptance into an instructional institution in the United States; fluency in English. Applicants must be nominated by an organization from their home countries that is funded or under consideration for funding by the Kellogg Foundation.
duration:	See description above
contact:	W. K. Kellogg Foundation International Study Grant Office One Michigan Avenue East Battle Creek, MI 49017-4058/USA (616) 968-1611

Kennan Institute for Advanced Russian Studies, Woodrow Wilson Center

Kennan Institute Research Scholarships

Fellowships are available for research on topics in Russian studies and concerning the successor states of the Soviet Union.

qualifications:	Doctoral degree or doctoral candidacy (the dissertation successfully defended prior to taking residence at the institute) or equivalent professional experience
duration:	Three to nine months
stipend:	$2,500 per month
deadline:	October 1

contact:	Fellowships and Grants
	The Woodrow Wilson
	   International Center for Scholars
	The Kennan Institute
	   of Advanced Russian Studies
	370 L'Enfant Promenade, SW, Suite 704
	Washington, DC 20024/USA
	(202) 287-3400

Kennan Institute Short-Term Grants

Short-term grants are offered to scholars having a particular need for the library, archival, and other specialized resources of the Washington, D.C., area. Grant recipients are required to be in residence in Washington during the program.

qualifications:	Doctoral degree or doctoral candidacy near completion, or equivalent professional achievement
duration:	One month
stipend:	$80 per day
deadline:	December 1, March 1, June 1, and September 1
contact:	See address above

Korea Foundation

The Korea Foundation Fellowship for Korean Studies

The Korea Foundation offers fellowships for Korean studies to university professors, doctoral candidates, and other qualified professionals who wish to carry out in-depth research in Korea.

qualifications: University professors, researchers at research institutes, doctoral candidates, or other qualified professionals who have research projects in Korean studies in the humanities, social sciences, or arts. Recipients should be in residence in Korea and be engaged in the fellowship projects full time.

duration: Two to ten months, beginning between February and December of the calendar year in which the grant is awarded

stipend: Round-trip airfare to and from Korea; monthly stipend ranging from 800,000 won ($1,000) for doctoral candidates to 1,200,000 won ($1,500) for senior professors. Housing, research facilities, and private offices not provided.

applications available: Applications may be obtained from either the Korea Foundation or Korean diplomatic missions

deadline: July 31

contact:
Fellowship for Korean Studies
The Korea Foundation
C.P.O. Box 2147
Seoul/Korea
(82-2) 753-6553
FAX: (82-2) 757-2049
TELEX: KOFO K27738

Fellowship for Korean Studies
The Korea Foundation
526, 5-ga,
Namdaemun-no,
Chung-gu
Seoul/Korea

The Korea Foundation Fellowship for Korean-Language Training

The Korea Foundation offers fellowships for Korean-language training to university students, faculty members, and other qualified professionals who wish to learn Korean at a Korean university. Fellowships are to be carried out at one of the language institutes specified by the foundation, and fellows are expected to engage in language training full time.

qualifications: University students (undergraduate or graduate), faculty members, researchers at research institutes in the fields related to Korean studies, or other qualified professionals who work in institutions related to Korea. Applicants should have basic Korean-language ability; however, applicants who plan a long-term career in Korean studies are also considered even if they lack Korean-language skills. Candidates under the age of thirty are given priority.

duration: Six, nine, or twelve months

stipend: Tuition fee for the Korean-language training: Senior scholars: 800,000 won ($1,000); students: 500,000 won ($600)

deadline: July 31

contact: See address above

Joan B. Kroc Institute for International Peace Studies, University of Notre Dame

International Scholars Program

The Kroc Institute provides opportunities for foreign graduate students to work toward an M.A. in peace studies at the University of Notre Dame. Students live together in a community, sharing trips, discussions, films, and other activities. Previous participants have been from Latin America, Asia, Africa, the Middle East, Europe, the Soviet Union, and North America.

qualifications: Bachelor's degree or its equivalent before the beginning of the program; under the age of thirty; fluency in spoken and written English

duration: August through June of the following year

deadline: Mid-January

contact: International Scholars Program
Institute for International Peace Studies
P.O. Box 639
Notre Dame, IN 46556-0639/USA
(219) 239-5014

Henry Luce Foundation, Inc.

Luce Scholars Program

Fellowships for work in an Asian country are offered to recent college graduates who would not normally come in contact with Asia in the course of their careers. The Luce Scholars Program is experiential rather than academic.

qualifications: U.S. citizenship; bachelor's degree. Applicants must be no more than twenty-nine years old by the beginning of the program and must be nominated by one of the colleges or universities participating in the program.

duration: Late August until mid-July of the following year

deadline: Nomination by early December; interviews in late December or early January

contact: The Henry Luce Foundation, Inc.
111 West Fiftieth Street
New York, NY 10020/USA
(212) 489-7700

John D. and Catherine T. MacArthur Foundation

Program on Peace and International Cooperation

The program encourages exploration of peace and cooperation issues in the context of economic, technological, ecological, and political change.

qualifications:	Scholars, journalists, policy analysts, and others. Young women and men and non–U.S. researchers are especially encouraged to apply.
duration:	Up to eighteen months of research in an appropriate institutional setting
stipend:	$10,000 to $60,000 for an individual application; up to $120,000 for a two-person project
deadline:	February 1, with the fellowship beginning in January of the following year
contact:	Grants for Research and Writing in Peace, Security, and International Cooperation The John D. and Catherine T. MacArthur Foundation 140 South Dearborn Street Chicago, IL 60603/USA (312) 726-8000

MacArthur Fellows Program

This program provides unique, unrestricted fellowships to exceptionally talented and promising individuals who have given evidence of originality, dedication to creative pursuits, and capacity for self-direction. Funding is provided in quarterly installments for five years to allow fellows the freedom to pursue their endeavors without time or financial constraints. The fellowships are administered without project proposals or applications, and without evaluation or the expectation of specific products or reports of any kind. The fellowships are intended to support individuals, not projects.

qualifications:	U.S. citizenship or residency; no restrictions as to discipline of expertise or profession. Candidates must be nominated by one of the designated nominators in the United States who serve their one-year terms anonymously; applications and informal nominations are not accepted.
duration:	Five years
stipend:	$30,000 to $75,000 annually, dependent on age
deadline:	None
contact:	See address above

Mershon Center, Ohio State University

Postdoctoral Fellowship for Research in International Security Studies

One postdoctoral fellowship is awarded for research in international security studies, including U.S. defense and foreign policy, international conflict resolution, military history, and civil-military relations. The fellow must reside in the Columbus, Ohio, area and work at the Mershon Center during the appointment.

qualifications: Doctorate awarded within five years prior to application from an institution other than Ohio State University

duration: Twelve months, beginning July 1

stipend: Approximately $29,000 per year

deadline: November 15

contact: Fellowship Coordinator
Mershon Center
Ohio State University
199 West Tenth Avenue
Columbus, OH 43201-2399/USA
(614) 292-1681

Government of Mexico

Mexican Government Scholarships

Scholarships are offered to U.S. citizens who wish to enroll in graduate programs in Mexico. Applicants should already have contacted or been accepted by the Mexican institution where they plan to study. If the scholarship is requested for a research project, a detailed description must be submitted with the application.

qualifications: Bachelor's degree; proficiency in Spanish

duration: Two years

stipend: Master's level: 265,000 pesos monthly; doctoral level: 285,000 pesos monthly; insurance

contact: Minister in Charge of Cultural Affairs
Mexican Embassy
2829 Sixteenth Street, NW
Washington, DC 20009/USA
(202) 234-6000

The National Academy of Sciences, National Research Council

Ford Foundation Postdoctoral Fellowship for Minorities

Funded by the Ford Foundation, the National Research Council sponsors fellowships to assist previously underrepresented minorities to pursue postdoctoral research in an environment free of interference from normal professional duties. The fellowships are intended to help gain greater recognition for young teacher-scholars who are either preparing for or are already engaged in university teaching in a wide variety of disciplines.

qualifications:	U.S. citizens or nationals who are members of the minority groups designated by the Ford Foundation and the National Research Council; Ph.D.
stipend:	$25,000 plus additional travel and relocation allowance
deadline:	Mid-January
contact:	Fellowship Office, National Research Council 2101 Constitution Avenue Washington, DC 20418/USA (202) 334-2860

National Association for Foreign Student Affairs (NAFSA)

NAFSA China Study Missions

Awards are offered to familiarize education personnel with and to stimulate interest in Chinese-U.S. educational exchanges through study missions to institutions in the People's Republic of China. China's State Education Commission determines the host institution.

qualifications:	Members of NAFSA who have worked with Chinese students or scholars but have not visited China
deadline:	September, with notification in late October
contact:	Director, Field Service Program National Association for Foreign Student Affairs 1860 Nineteenth Street, NW Washington, DC 20009/USA (202) 462-4811

National Council for Soviet and East European Research

Annual Research Competition

The council sponsors research on conditions in the former Soviet Union and Eastern Europe. Studies may concentrate on the social, political, economic, and historical development of the region; the council changes the topics annually.

qualifications:	U.S. citizenship or permanent residency; doctoral degree or equivalent experience
duration:	Up to fifteen months
stipend:	Up to $75,000 but usually less
deadline:	November 1
contact:	The National Council for Soviet and East European Research 1755 Massachusetts Avenue, NW Washington, DC 20036/USA (202) 387-0168

National Endowment for the Humanities (NEH)

The NEH is an independent grant-making agency of the federal government that supports research, education, and public programs in the humanities. In addition to the fellowships and grants highlighted below, the NEH also sponsors programs for research, study, travel, and seminars. For more information, contact the address below.

contact: National Endowment for the Humanities
1100 Pennsylvania Avenue, NW, Room 316
Washington, DC 20506/USA
(202) 786-0466

Fellowships for University Professors

Grants are provided to support full-time independent research in the humanities by the faculty of Ph.D.-granting universities.

qualifications: Individual faculty members from Ph.D.-granting universities

deadline: June 1

contact: See address above

Fellowships for College Teachers and Independent Scholars

These fellowships are designated for teachers from two-year, four-year, and five-year colleges and universities that do not maintain a doctoral program; independent scholars; and employees of schools, museums, and libraries. The program is for full-time independent study and research in the humanities.

deadline: June 1

contact: See address above

Study Grants for College and University Teachers

The program is intended to allow teachers with heavy teaching responsibilities the opportunity to participate in intensive study to increase their knowledge of their disciplines and the humanities. The fellowship is for study, not research, to assist in publication.

qualifications: College and university faculty with extensive teaching responsibilities

duration: Six weeks

deadline: August 15

contact: See address above

Faculty Graduate Study Program for Historically Black Colleges and Universities

Grants provide for full-time study culminating in a doctoral degree in the humanities.

qualifications: Faculty members at historically black colleges and universities, with preference given to doctoral candidates at the dissertation stage of their work. Grants are made through the applicant's institution.

duration: One year

deadline: Mid-March

contact: See address above

Summer Stipends

The grants provide support for full-time independent study and research.

qualifications: College and university teachers and individuals employed by schools, museums, and libraries. Applicants from colleges or universities must be nominated by their institutions.

duration: Two consecutive summer months

deadline: October 1

contact: See address above

National Science Foundation

Social and Economic Science Division Research Projects

Awards for research projects are made in the following areas: decision, risk, and management science; economics; geography and regional science; law and social science; methodology, measurement, and statistics in the social sciences; political science; and sociology. Grants are generally given to academic institutions and nonprofit research groups, although on occasion grants are provided to other types of institutions and individuals. Funding may be awarded for periods up to four and a half years, contingent upon the availability of funds and satisfactory progress of the research.

duration: Up to four and a half years

deadline: None. For review within six months, proposals should be submitted in line with target dates, which vary by division and program.

contact: Division Director
Social and Economic Science Division
National Science Foundation
Washington, DC 20550/USA
(202) 357-9857

National Security Education Program (NSEP), U.S. Department of Defense

National Security Scholarships, Fellowships, and Grants

The NSEP was founded in late 1991 to increase student involvement in less commonly taught languages, area studies, and other international fields. Plans are being made to offer scholarships for undergraduate students to study overseas, fellowships for graduate students, and grants to institutions of higher education to increase the study of international fields. The program funds scholars and fellows with the stipulation that upon completion of the student's education, he or she will work for the federal government or in the field of education as a form of repayment. As of April 1994, the qualifications and terms of the program had not yet been announced. NSEP coordinators can be contacted on most college campuses for applications and current information. Contact the address below for further information.

contact: National Security Education Program
P.O. Box 47103
Washington, DC 20050-7103/USA
(703) 696-1991

Friedrich Naumann Foundation

Research fellowships are awarded to German nationals. For more information contact the foundation office in Germany.

contact: Friedrich Naumann Foundation
Margarethenhof
53639 Königswinter/Germany
(49-0-2223) 7010

North Atlantic Treaty Organization (NATO)

Advanced Research Fellowship Programs

This program provides for research on issues relevant to NATO and its member nations.

qualifications: Working knowledge of the language of the applicant's target nation and have completion of doctoral-level work or its equivalent at the time of the application. Citizens of NATO nations must apply to their respective countries.

stipend: Up to BF 240,000

deadline: January 1

contact: Council for International Exchange of Scholars
3400 International Drive, NW, Suite M-500
Washington, DC 20008-3097/USA
(202) 686-6240

NATO Research Grants in the Sciences

This program provides two to four individual advanced fellowships annually for research on political, security, and economic issues directly affecting the health of the NATO alliance. Fellows conduct research in one or more NATO nations other than the United States in close cooperation with academic, research, or professional institutions.

qualifications: Completion of graduate studies in political, security, or economic disciplines

deadline: November 1

contact: See address above

Democratic Institutions Fellowship

This program was designed to foster research on democratic institutions and their functioning. The program comprises both individual and institutional fellowships.

qualifications: Citizens and residents of non-NATO countries of the North Atlantic Cooperation Council (NACC)

stipend: BF 240,000, inclusive of all travel costs

deadline: December 31

contact: The Office of Information and Press
Democratic Institutions Fellowships Programme
NATO
1110 Bruxelles/Belgium

Norwegian Nobel Institute

Norwegian Nobel Institute Fellowships

The Norwegian Nobel Institute awards several fellowships under its guest research program. The senior fellowship is awarded to a distinguished scholar with a substantial record of publications. The amount of each stipend is dependent on the individual's needs and on the availability of funds. The institute also covers travel expenses and some research and office equipment. Fellows are expected to devote themselves full time to writing and research and to be present at the institute. The senior fellow is expected to direct a research seminar at the institute for the other fellows in the program. The program's general theme has been "Great Powers, World Orders, and Interventions"; contact the institute for information about its current theme.

qualifications: Scholars of any nationality in the fields of history, social sciences, and international law. Projects can be historical or contemporary in their orientation.

stipend: See description above

contact: Dr. Odd Arne Westad, Research Director
The Norwegian Nobel Institute
Drammensveien 19
0255 Oslo/Norway
(47-2) 443680
FAX: (47-2) 430168

Office of Technology Assessment (OTA)

OTA Congressional Fellowship Program

This fellowship provides an opportunity for individuals to assist Congress in its deliberations of science and technology issues affecting public policy.

qualifications: Knowledge in areas including the physical or biological sciences, law, economics, environmental and social sciences, public policy, and engineering

duration: One year

stipend: $35,000 to $70,000 per year, based on the fellow's current salary, training, and experience

deadline: March 1

contact: Morris K. Udall Congressional Fellowships
Personnel Office
Office of Technology Assessment
Congress of the United States
Washington, DC 20510-8025/USA
(202) 224-8713

Organization of American States (OAS)

OAS Regular Training Program

The fundamental objective of the OAS is to further the economic, social, technical, and cultural development of the American peoples. Fellowships are available for advanced graduate study or research in an OAS member country.

qualifications:	Citizenship or permanent residency in an OAS member country; university degree and acceptance to a university, study center, or research site in the proposed host country. Applications must be submitted to the general secretariat through official channels established by each government.
duration:	Three months to two years
stipend:	Travel expenses, tuition fees, study materials, and a subsistence allowance
deadline:	March 1
contact:	General Secretariat of the Organization of American States Department of Fellowships and Training Trainee Selection Division Washington, DC 20006-4499/USA (202) 458-3000

Pew Trust Fellowship Programs

Pew Economic Freedom Fellows Program

The program is offered to individuals from countries previously under planned economies to study how market-oriented systems work in practical terms. Fellows participate in academic course work, structured internships, and firsthand observation of U.S. government and industry. The program is sponsored by the Pew Charitable Trusts and the Edmund A. Walsh School of Foreign Service of Georgetown University.

qualifications: Applicants must be between twenty-five and forty, have had experience in their countries' economic affairs, and appear destined for a leadership role as their countries move toward free market economies. All applications must be endorsed by the department or organization with which the candidate is affiliated.

duration: Five months

deadline: Late July

contact: Dr. Stuart S. Brown, Director
The Pew Economic Freedom Fellows Program
School of Foreign Service
Georgetown University
Washington, DC 20057/USA
(202) 687-5763

The Pew Faculty Fellowship in International Affairs

This program provides faculty from leading universities with instruction in the case method and support for case teaching. Fellows participate in an intensive two-week summer program at the John F. Kennedy School of Government and then use the skills learned in case teaching, writing, and course design to teach an international affairs course.

qualifications: Full-time faculty at accredited institutions who teach international affairs courses in political science, economics, or history

duration: One year

stipend: $9,000

deadline: February 1; awards announced in March

contact: John Boehrer, Director
The Pew Faculty Fellowship
   in International Affairs
John F. Kennedy School of Government
79 John F. Kennedy Street
Cambridge, MA 02138/USA
(617) 495-8295

Presidential Management Internship Program (PMI), U.S. Office of Personnel Management

The program aims to "attract to the Federal service outstanding individuals from a variety of academic disciplines who have a clear interest in, and commitment to, a career in the analysis and management of public policies and programs." Internships are intended to be the starting point for individuals wishing to pursue a career in federal service.

qualifications: U.S. citizenship and completion of advanced degree in the year of nomination. Applicants must be nominated by the college or university official who has an appropriate knowledge of the nominee's abilities and achievements.

duration: Two years

stipend: GS-9 ($25,700 per year) plus insurance and benefits

applications available: At graduate schools in the early fall

contact: Office of Personnel Management
Attn: PMI Program
1900 E Street, NW, Room 6336
Washington, DC 20415-0001/USA
(202) 504-2622

Resources for the Future (RFF)

Postdoctoral Fellowship Program

This program provides in-residence fellowships for intensive research in areas relating to the environment, natural resources, and energy.

qualifications: All nationalities; completion of doctorate within three to five years prior to application

duration: Two to ten months

deadline: March 1

applications available: November 1

contact: Chris Mendes
Resources for the Future
1616 P Street, NW
Washington, DC 20036/USA
(202) 328-5067

The RFF Small Grants Program

Grants are offered for projects generally concentrating on issues relating to the environment, natural resources, or energy. The RFF Small Grants Program provides start-up funding for new projects or supplementary support to complete specific aspects of ongoing projects.

qualifications: Researchers of all nationalities, but grants can be made only through tax-exempt institutions

duration: Two months to two years

stipend: Maximum $30,000

deadline: March 1

applications available: November 1

contact: See address above

Rhodes Scholarship Trust

Rhodes Scholarships

Thirty-two scholarships are offered annually to U.S. students for study at one of the colleges of Oxford University in Great Britain. Programs lead to the honors bachelor of arts, bachelor of philosophy, or master of philosophy.

qualifications: Scholars should be "physically, intellectually, and morally capable of leadership." U.S. candidates must be unmarried U.S. citizens between eighteen and twenty-four and must have completed the bachelor's degree prior to residence in Oxford.

duration: Two years

deadline: Varies

applications available: From home university or contact address below

contact: Office of the American Secretary
Rhodes Scholarship Trust
Pomona College
Claremont, CA 91711/USA
(909) 621-8138

Rockefeller Foundation

Rockefeller Foundation Social Science Research Fellowships in Agriculture and in Population Studies

The Rockefeller Foundation sponsors fellowships for young North American and African social scientists to conduct collaborative research in agriculture or population studies at foreign institutions. The program is intended to increase the number of social scientists who have had experience working in multidisciplinary international organizations on agricultural or population aspects of development. Although the fellows usually work with senior social or biological scientists, they may be asked to design research projects or fill roles not previously represented at the host institution.

qualifications:	Canadian or U.S. citizenship or permanent residency; Ph.D. within four years prior to the application. African social scientists are also eligible to apply for positions at institutions in the United States and Canada.
stipend:	A stipend, health insurance, international travel, and the shipment of personal belongings
deadline:	December 31
contact:	Manager, Fellowship Office Rockefeller Foundation 1133 Avenue of the Americas New York, NY 10036/USA (212) 869-8500

African Dissertation Internship Awards

The program enables Ph.D. students from sub-Saharan Africa enrolled in U.S. and Canadian universities to return to Africa for extensive field research in areas relevant to economic development or poverty alleviation. Priority is given to research topics in the fields of agriculture, health, and life sciences, but other proposals are welcome. Applicants are responsible for arranging affiliation with an African institution able to provide needed research support such as laboratory facilities, access to study sites, and technical advice. The candidate's faculty advisor, the host institution in Africa, and the agency with primary responsibility for financing the student's graduate work must all send letters of endorsement.

qualifications: African nationals enrolled in doctoral degree programs at U.S. or Canadian universities

stipend: $18,500 to $35,000

deadline: March 1 and October 1; candidates should apply well in advance of the expected fieldwork starting date

contact: African Dissertation Internship Awards
Special Programming Grants
International Program to
  Support Science-Based Development
Rockefeller Foundation
1133 Avenue of the Americas
New York, NY 10036/USA
(202) 869-8500

Rotary Foundation

Rotary Grants for University Teachers to Serve in Developing Countries

Grants are offered to university teachers to teach a subject of practical use in a country with a per capita GNP of $5,999 or less.

qualifications: Applicants must have held a college or university appointment for three or more years; a specific rank is not required. Although acceptance is not affected by membership in the Rotary Club, the country of the applicant's present academic post and of the proposed teaching position must both contain at least one Rotary Club. Applicants may not have previously received a Rotary Foundation teaching grant. Proficiency in the language of the host country is considered in the selection process.

duration: Three to ten months

stipend: $10,000 for three to five months; $20,000 for six to ten months

deadline: June 1 of year preceding fellowship

contact: Either the local chapter of the Rotary Club or:
The Rotary Foundation of Rotary International
One Rotary Center
1560 Sherman Avenue
Evanston, IL 60201/USA
(708) 866-3000 x 3424
FAX: (708) 328-8281

Graduate Scholarships

Scholarships are offered to promote international understanding and goodwill through study in a country that has a Rotary Club.

qualifications:	Bachelor's degree or its equivalent, enrollment in studies at the graduate level, and proficiency in the language of the host country. Citizens from any of the 164 countries in which there is a Rotary Club are eligible.
duration:	Nine months
stipend:	Tuition, travel, living expenses, academic fees, and some educational supplies
deadline:	Set by local Rotary Clubs and districts
contact:	Either the local chapter of the Rotary Club or: Margaret Omori, Supervisor, Scholarships Awards Section at the address above

International Peace Scholarships

Scholarships are awarded to promote international understanding and goodwill through study at an institution selected by the Rotary Foundation. The university hosting the program changes annually; in the past the program has taken place at the University of Hong Kong and Griffith University in Nathan, Australia. The program concentrates in peace studies, conflict resolution, and international relations.

qualifications:	Students at the undergraduate and graduate levels who are citizens of one of the 164 countries that has a Rotary Club. Candidates are chosen by district selection committees and one scholarship winner is selected from each of the six Rotary regions in the world.
deadline:	Set by local Rotary Clubs and districts
contact:	Either the local chapter of the Rotary Club or: Theresa A. Nissen, Scholarship Programs, Competitive Awards at the address above

Rothmans Foundation

Rothmans Fellowships

The Rothmans Foundation awards fellowships for research at an Australian university or institution.

qualifications:	Three years' postgraduate research experience in any field; must begin the fellowship before turning thirty years old
duration:	One year with extension possible
stipend:	Up to $25,000
deadline:	July 29
contact:	Rothmans Foundation 139 Macquarie Street, Seventh Floor Sydney NSW 2000/Australia

Saitama University, Institute for Policy Science

Research Fellowships

One research fellowship, at the Institute for Policy Science, is made available each year to a non–Japanese scholar. The fellowship concentrates on energy problems, national security, the decisionmaking system of the Japanese government, and other topics.

qualifications:	Strong social science or engineering background, Ph.D. preferred; citizenship in any country, excluding Japan
duration:	September through the following August
stipend:	258,000 yen to 514,000 yen (approximately $1,120 to $2,230) per month, plus expenses for travel from the fellow's home country to Tokyo
deadline:	February 15
contact:	Professor Fumio Kodama Institute for Policy Science Saitama University Urawa Saitama 338/Japan

School of Advanced International Studies (SAIS), Johns Hopkins University

Hopkins-Nanjing Program Scholarships

Scholarships are awarded to permit study at the Hopkins-Nanjing University Center for Chinese and American Studies in Nanjing, the People's Republic of China. Scholars should be working in Chinese studies in the areas of history, foreign policy, international relations, and economics.

qualifications:	Graduate students, postdoctoral scholars, and professionals who are citizens of the United States
duration:	One year
stipend:	Tuition, travel, and living expenses
deadline:	February 1
contact:	William Speidel, Executive Director School of Advanced International Studies 1619 Massachusetts Avenue, NW Washington, DC 20036/USA (202) 663-5800 FAX: (202) 663-5891

SAIS and Bologna Center Fellowships

Fellowships are available to permit study at SAIS in Washington, D.C., or Bologna, Italy.

qualifications:	Graduate students specializing in international relations
duration:	One year
stipend:	Tuition
deadline:	March 1
contact:	Priscilla Rossetti, Director Financial Aid Office School of Advanced International Studies 1740 Massachusetts Avenue, NW Washington, DC 20036/USA (202) 663-5706 FAX: (202) 663-5639

School of Oriental and African Studies, University of London

Scholarship

Scholarships are awarded to support study for a master's degree at the University of London School of Oriental and African Studies. Recipients should be involved in the fields of Oriental studies, African studies, Oriental languages, or African languages.

qualifications: Scholars of Oriental and African societies and languages

stipend: About $6,500

deadline: May 1; notification by July 1

contact: J. T. Bishop, Registrar
Thornhaugh Street, Russell Square
London WC1H 0XG/England
(44-1) 637-2388

School of Public Affairs, University of Maryland at College Park

Advanced Seminar on the U.S. Foreign Policy Process

Funded by the Ford Foundation, this annual seminar enables fellows, primarily from developing countries, to engage in direct, intensive analysis of the U.S. foreign policy process through academic courses, contact with the Washington policy community, and research.

qualifications: Midcareer government officials, policy-oriented scholars, and journalists who have demonstrated analytical skills on foreign policy issues and have several years of policy-relevant experience. Fellowships are for non–U.S. citizens only.

duration: January through May

deadline: September 1

contact: Maryland Seminar on
U.S. Foreign Policy Making
Center for International
and Security Studies at Maryland
School of Public Affairs, University of Maryland
College Park, MD 20742/USA
(301) 405-7601

Scoville Peace Fellowship Program

Herbert Scoville Peace Fellowship

This fellowship is designed to give college graduates an opportunity to work on issues of peace and arms control at an organization in Washington, D.C. Topics include disarmament, arms control, the military budget, and U.S. relations with the former Soviet republics.

qualifications:	Bachelor's degree; preferably a strong interest in arms control and experience in peace issues outside of Washington, D.C. Applications from women, minorities, and graduates of schools without major arms control and peace programs are welcome.
duration:	Four to six months
stipend:	$1,200 per month
deadline:	October 15 for spring semester; March 15 for fall semester
contact:	Scoville Peace Fellowship Program 110 Maryland Avenue, NE, Room 409 Washington, DC 20002/USA (202) 543-4100

Hanns Seidel Foundation

Research fellowships are awarded to German nationals. For more information contact the foundation office in Germany.

contact:	Hanns Seidel Foundation Lazarettstrasse 33 80636 Munich/Germany (49-0-89) 12580

Social Science Research Council (SSRC)

In addition to the general fellowships listed below, SSRC also offers fellowships for study on or in sub-Saharan Africa, China, Eastern Europe, Japan, Korea, Latin America and the Caribbean, the Near and Middle East, South Asia, Southeast Asia, the former Soviet Union and its successor states, Western Europe, Afghanistan, and Central Asia. For more information on these and other SSRC programs, contact the address below.

contact: Social Science Research Council
605 Third Avenue
New York, NY 10158/USA
(212) 661-0280
FAX: (212) 370-7896

SSRC-MacArthur Foundation Fellowships of Peace and Security in a Changing World

Dissertation and postdoctoral fellowships are offered to support research on the implications for security issues of worldwide cultural, social, economic, and political changes. Various issues are acceptable, although they must be linked to topics in peace and security. Fellowships do not support an extension or expansion of an applicant's research; the research proposal must exhibit a significant departure from previous work. Dissertation fellowships pay a stipend appropriate for the cost of living in the area where the fellow will be working, rarely exceeding $17,500 per year. Postdoctoral fellowships pay a stipend appropriate for the fellow's current salary and the cost of living in the area where the fellow will be working, rarely exceeding $36,000 per year.

qualifications: Researchers in the social and behavioral sciences, the humanities, or the physical and biological sciences. An academic appointment is not required either for application or during the fellowship term. Dissertation fellowship applicants must have completed all requirements for their doctorates minus the dissertations by the time of the announcement of the awards. Postdoctoral fellows must have their Ph.D.'s or equivalent degrees or comparable research experience and an ability to contribute to the research literature. Senior researchers are discouraged from applying.

duration: Two years
stipend: See description above
deadline: December 1
contact: See address above

International Peace and Security: Visiting Scholar Fellowships

Fellowships are offered to scholars and researchers to conduct research at universities and research centers outside their home regions. In recent years fellowships have been offered primarily to researchers from Africa, Eastern Europe, Central Europe, and the non-Russian successors of the Soviet Union. Proposals that focus on the effects of recent changes in the international political and economic systems on cultural, social, economic, political, military, or environmental conditions of Africa and Eastern or Central Europe are encouraged.

qualifications: Postdoctoral researchers, junior faculty, or lawyers, journalists, and others with comparable research experience. Applicants must be nationals of Eastern or Central Europe or Africa. Recent Ph.D. recipients (within seven years prior to application) encouraged to apply.
duration: Three months
deadline: July 15; awards announced in November
contact: See address above

Joint International Fellowship and Grant Programs for Area and Comparative Training and Research

The SSRC, in collaboration with the American Council of Learned Societies (ACLS), sponsors fellowships to increase predissertation, dissertation, and postdoctoral research in distinctive areas, cultures, languages, and historical experiences. The organizations also hope to promote comparative and transnational analysis based on area expertise. Predissertation research is intended to assist graduate students in the areas of economics, political science, and sociology who would consider doing a dissertation in a developing country but need additional training to do so. Fellowships to fund doctoral dissertation research are administered by the area programs of SSRC and ACLS. Postdoctoral research should focus on a country or an area or on comparisons across countries or areas.

qualifications:	U.S. citizenship or three years of consecutive residency in the United States. Predissertation Fellowships: Applicants must be graduate students. Dissertation Fellowships for Area Research: Applicants must be full-time doctoral students, regardless of citizenship. Fellowships are for nine to eighteen consecutive months of field research. Grants for Advanced Area and Comparative Research: Applicants must hold a Ph.D. or its equivalent.
stipend:	Varies by academic level and location of fellowship
deadline:	Varies by region of study
applications available:	September
contact:	See address above

For information about Area Programs in Eastern Europe or China, contact the ACLS at the address listed under the ACLS in this guide.

International Predissertation Fellowship Program

This fellowship provides support for language training, overseas study, and course work in area studies in order to promote interdisciplinary and cross-regional dialogue on theoretical as well as methodological issues. The program is aimed primarily at graduate students in economics, political science, and sociology, but it is open to students in other disciplines as well.

qualifications:	Doctoral candidates from the twenty-three specified universities are eligible; for a list of the universities, contact SSRC. Students should be in the early phases of their training.
duration:	Twelve months
applications available:	September
contact:	See address above

Abe Fellowship

The SSRC and the ACLS jointly administer this fellowship funded by the Japan Foundation Center for Global Peace. The fellowship is intended to support policy-relevant research on Japan and the United States beyond the work of single-country specialists and to extend the scope of traditional Japanese and American studies through the incorporation of international and comparative perspectives. Applications are accepted from scholars and nonacademic research professionals to conduct research in global issues, problems common to advanced industrial societies, and issues that relate to improving Japan-U.S. relations.

qualifications: Japanese and U.S. research professionals with a doctorate-equivalent level of professional training; third-country nationals affiliated with U.S. or Japanese institutions. Previous language training is not a prerequisite.

deadline: September 1

contact: See address above

Soros Foundations

The Soros network of foundations supports Central and Eastern European projects and people. While the scope of each foundation's programs is usually local, the foundations cooperate on a number of regional projects. The foundations are mainly interested in education, culture, civil society, health, and the environment and seek to provide educational opportunities for individuals.

Democratic Infrastructure Grants

Grants are awarded to organizations or individuals for legal reform; assisting a democratic and independent media; encouraging pluralism, human rights, and voter participation; and promoting the development of the not-for-profit sector.

qualifications:	Citizenship in countries in Central and Eastern Europe or the former Soviet Union; nonresidency in the West
deadline:	None
contact:	Soros Foundations 888 Seventh Avenue, Suite 1901 New York, NY 10106/USA (212) 757-2323 FAX: (212) 974-0367

Soros Scholarships and Fellowships

Soros Scholarships and Fellowships are awarded for study at Oxford University, American University in Bulgaria, the International Management Center (Budapest), the U.S. Library of Congress, and other institutions where named programs have been established.

qualifications:	Citizenship in countries in Central and Eastern Europe or the former Soviet Union; nonresidency in the West
deadline:	Varies; contact the Soros Foundation office in your country of origin
contact:	See address above

Supplementary Grants Program

The Soros Supplementary Grants Program enables students from Central and Eastern Europe and the republics of the former Soviet Union to take advantage of Western scholarships. Specifically, students who have been awarded a full scholarship (including tuition, room, and board) from an accredited Western college or university receive a grant for travel and/or an allowance for personal expenses (books, etc.) based on individual circumstances of financial need but in no case to exceed $2,500.

qualifications: Citizenship in Central and Eastern Europe or the former Soviet Union; nonresidency in the West. Supplementary grants are awarded only to those with full scholarships and only for the first year of study. Recipients of Fulbright, Tempus, or Erasmus Program scholarships are not eligible.

stipend: Up to $2,500

deadline: None; applications must be received at least six weeks before the course of study is to begin

contact: See address above

United Nations

United Nations Institute for Training and Research (UNITAR) Fellowships

Fellowships are awarded to nationals of developing countries with law degrees and practical experience in international law. The fellowships, offered in The Hague, Geneva, or New York in conjunction with The Hague Academy of International Law and the International Court of Justice, provide practical training in United Nations offices dealing with legal matters.

qualifications: Nationals of developing countries, between the ages of twenty-four and forty, with experience in international law and a good command of English or French

deadline: April 1

contact: Direct correspondence, through the appropriate official government channels, to the Director of Training, UNITAR, or write to the following address:
United Nations Institute for
  Training and Research
United Nations Office at Geneva
Palais de Nations
1211 Geneva 10/Switzerland

United States Department of Education

The U.S. Department of Education sponsors programs that give funding to academic institutions to be disbursed to qualified faculty and scholars. Contact home academic institutions for information about government-funded programs (such as Fulbright-Hayes).

Jacob Javits Fellows Program

The Department of Education sponsors fellowships for graduate study in the arts, humanities, or social sciences. To continue receiving financial support the fellow must show evidence of satisfactory progress.

qualifications: Graduating seniors and first-year graduate students with twenty or fewer graduate credit hours

duration: Up to forty-eight months

stipend: Contingent upon financial need; up to $10,000 plus $6,000 for fees, tuition, and educational expenses

deadline: January 18

contact: Division of Higher Education Incentive Programs
Office of Post-secondary Education
U.S. Department of Education
Washington, DC 20202-5251/USA
(202) 708-9415

or for an application:
Jacob K. Javits Fellowship Program
P.O. Box 84
Washington, DC 20044/USA
(800) 4FED-AID
(800) 433-3242

United States Information Agency (USIA)

Fulbright Program Award in Japan for U.S. Nationals

Scholarships are awarded to support visiting lecturers, research scholars, and graduate students from the United States in Japan. USIA encourages applications dealing with Japanese studies, international education, Japanese language, natural and applied sciences, problems of contemporary society, and political and economic relations in the Pacific.

qualifications: U.S. citizenship; graduate students, postdoctoral scholars, and professionals

duration: Three months to one year

stipend: 200,000 to 430,000 yen per month

deadline: October 31

contact: U.S. Student Programs Division
Institute of International Education
809 United Nations Plaza
New York, NY 10017-3580/USA
(212) 883-8200
FAX: (212) 984-5452

Fulbright Scholar Program

Awards and fellowships are given for research and/or lecturing in various disciplines at universities in foreign countries.

qualifications: U.S. citizenship. For lecturing positions, a doctorate and postdoctoral teaching experience are required. Research applicants must have a doctorate or equivalent degree. Junior lecturing and research programs are designed primarily for young scholars who are recent Ph.D.'s or advanced Ph.D. candidates. In some cases foreign-language proficiency is recommended.

deadline: Varies by region of interest; contact the USIA for more information

contact: See address above

International applicants should contact the Fulbright Association in their home countries.

United States Institute of Peace (USIP)

Jennings Randolph Program for International Peace

All Jennings Randolph Fellowships are for research at the USIP.

Distinguished fellows: Awards are intended for political leaders, scholars, and other professionals who have achieved national or international stature by virtue of extraordinary scholarly or practical achievements in peace and conflict management or related fields. Stipends are determined individually in relation to earned income for the preceding twelve months but cannot exceed the GS-15/10 level of the federal pay scale.

Peace fellows: These fellowships are available for scholars and other professionals who demonstrate substantial accomplishment or promise of exceptional leadership. Stipends are determined individually but cannot exceed the GS-15/1 level of the federal pay scale.

Peace scholars: Awards are intended for outstanding students in recognized doctoral programs at U.S. universities. The fellowships enable them to devote their dissertation research to topics that advance the state of knowledge or education about international peace and conflict management. Stipends for Peace scholars are currently set at $14,000 per year and are paid directly to the individual.

qualifications:	All nationalities; all professional backgrounds and academic disciplines
duration:	One year
stipend:	See description above
deadlines:	Distinguished fellows: October 15; Peace fellows: October 15; Peace scholars: November 15
contact:	United States Institute of Peace Jennings Randolph Program for International Peace 1550 M Street, NW, Suite 700 Washington, DC 20005-1708/USA (202) 457-1700 FAX: (202) 429-6063

Solicited and Unsolicited Grants Program

The USIP sponsors grants for solicited and unsolicited projects in civil and military relations, administration of justice and the rule of law, international and regional organizations and conflict management, and demobilization and peacekeeping.

qualifications: Nonprofit organizations, official public institutions, and individuals

stipend: $32,000 average

deadline: January 2

contact: Solicited Grants Project
Office of Public Affairs
United States Institute of Peace
1550 M Street, NW, Suite 700-CH
Washington, DC 20005-1708/USA
(202) 457-1700
FAX: (202) 429-6063

University of Maryland, College Park

Scholarships for Adult Women

Scholarships, funded by the Charlotte W. Newcombe Foundation, are available through the Returning Students Program to non-traditional-age undergraduate students at the University of Maryland, College Park campus.

qualifications: Women must be twenty-five years or older; be admitted as full- or part-time undergraduate students at the University of Maryland, College Park, day school; and have demonstrated their academic ability and a commitment to their educational goals by having completed at least half of the credits necessary for a degree. Special consideration is given to women with verifiable financial need and women with disabilities.

stipend: Partial tuition expenses as well as the cost of any off-campus supervised internship, books and fees, child-care costs, or any career-related costs

deadline: Mid-July

contact: Beverly Greenfeig or Barbara Goldberg
Returning Students Program
University of Maryland's Counseling Center
University of Maryland
College Park, MD 20742/USA
(301) 314-7693

For other programs at the University of Maryland at College Park, see also Institutional Reform and the Informal Sector and School of Public Affairs.

Volkswagen Foundation

"Central and Eastern Europe" Academic Program: Grants for Junior Researchers

The Volkswagen Foundation sponsors fellowships for young researchers to support the construction and reconstruction of science in the former socialist countries of Bulgaria, the Czech Republic, Estonia, Hungary, Latvia, Lithuania, Poland, Romania, and the Slovak Republic. The fellowships provide opportunities to do research at German universities; fellows are also expected to participate in teaching. The humanities and social sciences are given priority.

qualifications: Invitation by a German institute of higher learning to join the faculty for the duration of the term. Applications should be submitted to the German Academy of Sciences by instructors at institutes of higher learning in the Federal Republic of Germany.

duration: Six months

contact: Konferenz der Deutschen Akademien der Wissenschaften
Kennwort: Stipendienprogramm Mittel- und Osteuropa
Geschwister-Scholl-Strasse 2
55131 Mainz/Germany
(49-0-6131) 57-37-35
FAX: (49-0-6131) 51-31-6

White House Fellows

The fellowships offer an opportunity for individuals to work within the government in the Executive Office of the President or in an executive branch department or agency. As a government employee, each fellow is paid by his or her agency at an appropriate level based on experience and education at a rate not higher rate than GS-15, step 3.

qualifications: U.S. citizens who work in any field; previous professional experience is generally not related to the responsibilities associated with the fellowship program. While there is no specific age limit, the fellowship is intended for individuals in the early and formative years of their careers. Employees of the federal government (except career military personnel) are ineligible.

duration: September through August of the following year

stipend: See description above

deadline: Mid-December

contact: Commission on White House Fellowships
712 Jackson Place, NW
Washington, DC 20503/USA
(202) 395-4522

Woodrow Wilson International Center for Scholars

Woodrow Wilson Center Fellowships

Fellowships are available to researchers for original research or participation in one of the center's programs (the Asia Program; the East and West European Program; the History, Culture, and Society Program; the International Studies Program; the Kennan Institute for Advanced Russian Studies; the Latin American Program; the United States Program).

qualifications:	Doctoral degree and extensive postdissertation publications or equivalent professional experience
duration:	Four months to one academic year
stipend:	Average of $38,000 yearly
deadline:	October 1
contact:	The Fellowships Office The Woodrow Wilson Center Washington, DC 20560/USA (202) 667-0417

Woodrow Wilson National Fellowship Foundation

Charlotte W. Newcombe
Doctoral Dissertation Fellowships

This fellowship provides the opportunity to write on ethical or religious values. Suggested areas include the ethical implications of foreign policy, the values influencing political decisions, the moral codes of other cultures, and religious or ethical issues reflected in history or literature.

qualifications:	Candidates for Ph.D., Th.D., or Ed.D. degrees in doctoral programs in the United States; fulfillment of all requirements, minus the dissertation, by the time of application
duration:	Twelve months of full-time dissertation writing, beginning in June or September
stipend:	$12,000
deadline:	Late November
contact:	Newcombe Dissertation Fellowships The Woodrow Wilson National Fellowship Foundation P.O. Box 642 Princeton, NJ 08542-0642/USA (609) 924-4666

Women in Government Relations Leader Foundation

Fellowships/Grants-in-Aid

This program provides opportunities for advanced educational and leadership training to midcareer women with experience in business or government relations.

qualifications:	Five years of full-time professional experience in business or government relations
stipend:	$5,000 for full-time students

contacts:

Michele Isele
Citizens for a
  Sound Economy
470 L'Enfant Plaza, SW
East Building, Suite 7112
Washington, DC 20024/
  USA
(202) 488-8200

Susan Aaronson
The Brookings
  Institution
1775 Massachusetts
  Avenue, NW
Washington, DC
  20036/USA
(202) 797-6000
  x4019

Women's Research and Education Institute (WREI)

Congressional Fellowships on Women and Public Policy

The fellowships place graduate students in congressional offices and on committee staffs. Fellows spend thirty hours per week in their assigned offices and receive six hours of arranged credit for the legislative and academic research they perform.

qualifications:	Enrollment in a graduate or professional degree program. An interest in "the analysis of gender differences as they affect federal laws" is helpful.
duration:	One year
stipend:	Tuition and living stipend
deadline:	Mid-February
contact:	WREI Congressional Fellowships 1700 Eighteenth Street, NW, #400 Washington, DC 20009/USA (202) 328-7070

Carter G. Woodson Institute for Afro-American and African Studies, University of Virginia

Afro-American and African Studies Fellowship Programs

Fellowships are awarded for residential research in disciplines of the humanities and social sciences concerned with Afro-American and African studies, which is considered to cover Africa, Africans, and peoples of African descent in North, Central, and South America and the Caribbean, past and present. Fellows must be in residence at the University of Virginia for the duration of the award period and are expected to contribute to the intellectual life of the university. To this end, predoctoral fellows become visiting graduate students and postdoctoral fellows receive the status of visiting scholars.

qualifications:	For the predoctoral fellowships, completion of all requirements for the doctorate except the dissertation prior to August 1; for the post-doctoral fellowships, doctorate by the time of application or proof that the degree will have been received by June 30 prior to the beginning of the fellowship
duration:	Predoctoral fellowships: two years; postdoctoral fellowships: one year; both beginning August 1
stipend:	Predoctoral fellowships: $12,500 per year; postdoctoral fellowships: $25,000
deadline:	Early December; contact the institute for the specific date
contact:	Afro-American and African Studies Fellowship The Carter G. Woodson Institute University of Virginia 1512 Jefferson Park Avenue Charlottesville, VA 22903/USA (804) 924-3109

World Bank

Robert S. McNamara Fellowships Program

Postdoctoral fellowships are offered to support innovative research in areas of economic development. The program funds travel and living expenses for the fellows to study in a World Bank member country other than their own.

qualifications:	Nationals of World Bank member countries; thirty-five years old or younger; master's degree or equivalent by the time of application (the fellowship will not fund research toward an advanced degree); working knowledge of the language of the proposed host country. All requests for application forms must quote reference number RSM/93/1.
duration:	Twelve months
stipend:	$25,000 standard
deadline:	December 31
contact:	The Robert S. McNamara Fellowships Program World Bank Headquarters 1818 H Street, NW, Room M-4029 Washington, DC 20433/USA (202) 473-6441

World Bank Graduate Scholarship Program

With grant funding from the government of Japan, the World Bank has established scholarships for graduate studies leading to a higher degree in a development-related social science. The program is aimed at increasing the number of high-quality professionals in economic and social development.

qualifications: Applicants mainly from developing countries. Recipients are expected to return to their home countries at the conclusion of studies and apply the knowledge and skills acquired to help accelerate the pace of economic and social development.

stipend: Full tuition, the cost of medical and accident insurance obtained through the university, a monthly subsistence allowance for one person, and economy-class travel

deadline: March 1

contact: Administrator, Graduate Scholarship Program
World Bank Headquarters
1818 H Street, NW, Room M-4035
Washington, DC 20433/USA
(202) 473-6849

Zeta Phi Beta Sorority
National Education Foundation

General Graduate Fellowships

This program provides stipends to women who are working toward a professional, master's, doctorate, or postdoctoral degree.

qualifications: Distinction in the applicant's chosen field; membership in Zeta Phi Beta not required

stipend: Up to $25,000 per year

deadline: February 1

contact: Zeta Phi Beta National Headquarters
1734 New Hampshire Avenue, NW
Washington, DC 20009/USA
(202) 387-3103

Nancy B. Woolridge Fellowships

These fellowships are awarded to U.S. graduate students or undergraduates for academic study abroad and to foreign students for study within the United States.

qualifications: Documented proof of academic study and a course plan; membership in Zeta Phi Beta not required

deadline: February 1

contact: See address above

APPENDIXES

On the Art of Writing Proposals

Some Candid Suggestions for Applicants to Social Science Research Council Competitions

Adam Przeworski & Frank Salomon

WRITING PROPOSALS for research funding is a peculiar facet of North American academic culture, and as with all things cultural, its attributes rise only partly into public consciousness. A proposal's overt function is to persuade a committee of scholars that the project shines with the three kinds of merit all disciplines value, namely, conceptual innovation, methodological rigor, and rich, substantive content. But to make these points stick, a proposal writer needs a feel for the unspoken customs, norms, and needs that govern the selection process itself. These are not really as arcane or ritualistic as one might suspect. For the most part, these customs arise from the committee's efforts to deal in good faith with its own problems: incomprehension among disciplines, work overload, and the problem of equitably judging proposals that reflect unlike social and academic circumstances.

Writing for committee competition is an art quite different from research work itself. After long deliberation, a committee usually has to choose among proposals that all possess the three virtues mentioned above. Other things being equal, the proposal that is awarded funding is the one that gets its merits across more forcefully because it addresses these unspoken needs and norms as well as the overt rules. The purpose of these pages is to give competitors for Council fellowships and funding a more even start by making explicit some of those normally unspoken customs and needs.

Capture the Reviewer's Attention

While the form and the organization of a proposal are matters of taste, you should choose your form bearing in mind that

---

Copyright © 1988 by the Social Science Research Council, 605 Third Avenue, New York, NY 10158. Reprinted by permission.

every proposal reader constantly scans for clear answers to three questions:

- *What are we going to learn as the result of the proposed project that we do not know now?*
- *Why is it worth knowing?*
- *How will we know that the conclusions are valid?*

Working through a tall stack of proposals on voluntarily donated time, a committee member rarely has time to comb proposals for hidden answers. So, say what you have to say immediately, crisply, and forcefully. The opening paragraph, or the first page at most, is your chance to grab the reviewer's attention. Use it. This is the moment to overstate, rather than understate, your point or question. You can add the conditions and caveats later.

Questions that are clearly posed are an excellent way to begin a proposal: *Are strong party systems conducive to democratic stability? Was the decline of population growth in Brazil the result of government policies?* These should not be rhetorical questions; they have effect precisely because the answer is far from obvious. Stating your central point, hypothesis, or interpretation is also a good way to begin: *Workers do not organize unions; unions organize workers. The success, and failure, of Corazon Aquino's revolution stems from its middle class origins. Population growth coupled with loss of arable land poses a threat to North African food security in the 1990's.*

Obviously some projects are too complex and some conceptualizations too subtle for such telegraphic messages to capture. Sometimes only step-by-step argumentation can define the central problem. But even if you adopt this strategy, do not fail to leave the reviewer with something to remember: some message that will remain after reading many other proposals and discussing them for hours and hours. "She's the one who claims that *Argentina never had a liberal democratic tradition*" is how you want to be referred to during the committee's discussion, not "Oh yes, she's the one from Chicago."

Aim for Clarity

Remember that most proposals are reviewed by multidisciplinary committees. A reviewer studying a proposal from another field expects the proposer to meet her halfway. After all, the reader probably accepted the committee appointment because of the excitement of surveying other people's ideas. Her only reward is the chance that proposals will provide a lucidly guided tour of various disciplines' research frontiers. Don't cheat the reviewer of this by inflicting a tiresome trek through the duller idiosyncrasies of your discipline. Many disciplines have parochial traditions of writing in pretentious jargon. You should avoid jargon as much as you can, and when technical language is really needed, restrict yourself to those new words and technical terms that truly lack equivalents in common language. Also, keep the spotlight on ideas. An archaeologist should argue the concepts latent in the ceramic typology more than the typology itself, a historian the tendency latent in the mass of events, and so forth. When additional technical material is needed, or when the argument refers to complex ancillary material, putting it into appendices decongests the main text.

Establish the Context

Your proposal should tell the committee not only what will be learned as a result of your project, but what will be learned that somebody else does not already know. It is essential that the proposal summarize the current state of knowledge and provide an up-to-date, comprehensive bibliography. Both should be precise and succinct. They need not constitute a review of "the literature" but a sharply focused view of the specific body or bodies of knowledge to which you will add. Committees often treat bibliographies as a sign of seriousness on the part of the applicant, and some members will put considerable effort into evaluating them. A good bibliography testifies that the author did enough preparatory work to make sure the project will complement and not duplicate other people's efforts. Many proposals fail because the references are incomplete or outdated. Missing even a single reference can be very costly if it shows failure to connect with research directly relevant to one's own. Proposal writers with limited library resources are urged to correspond with colleagues and libraries elsewhere in the early stages of research planning. Resource guides such as *Dissertation Abstracts International* and *Social Science Periodical Index* are highly recommended.

For many disciplines, Annual Reviews (e.g., *Annual Review of Anthropology*) offer state of the art discussions and rich bibliographies. Some disciplines have bibliographically oriented journals, for example, *Review of Economic Literature* and *Contemporary Sociology*. There are also valuable area-studies-oriented guides: *Handbook of Latin American Studies, International African Bibliography,* etc. Familiarizing yourself with them can save days of research.

What's the Payoff?

Disciplinary norms and personal tastes in justifying research activities differ greatly. Some scholars are swayed by the statement that "it has not been studied" (e.g., an historian may argue that no book has been written about a particular event, and therefore one is needed), while other scholars sometimes reflect that there may be a good reason why not. Nevertheless, the fact that less is known about one's own chosen case, period, or country than about similar ones may work in the proposer's favor. Between two identical projects, save that one concerns Egypt and the other the Sudan, reviewers are likely to prefer the latter. Citing the importance of the events that provide the subject matter is another and perhaps less dubious appeal. "Turning points," "crucial breakthroughs," "central personages," "fundamental institutions," and similar appeals to the significance of the object of research are sometimes effective if argued rather than merely asserted. Appealing to current importance may also work: e.g., democratic consolidation in South America, the aging population in industrialized countries, the relative decline of the hegemony of the United States. It's crucial to convince readers that such topics are not merely timely, but that their current urgency provides a window into some more abiding problem.

Among many social scientists, explicit theoretical interest counts heavily as a point of merit. Theoretical exposition need not go back to the axiomatic bases of the discipline—proposal readers will have a reasonable interdisciplinary breadth—but it should situate the local problem in terms of its relevance to live, sometimes controversial, theoretical currents. Help your reader understand where the problem intersects the main theoretical debates in your field and show how this inquiry puts established ideas to the test or offers new ones. Good proposals demonstrate awareness of alternative viewpoints and argue the author's position in such a way as to address the field broadly, rather than developing a single sectarian tendency indifferent to alternatives.

Use a Fresh Approach

Surprises, puzzles, and apparent contradictions can powerfully persuade the reviewer whose disciplinary superego enforces a commitment to systematic model building or formal theorizing:

"Given its long-standing democratic traditions, Chile was expected to return to democracy before other countries in the Southern Cone and yet. . . . Is it because these traditions were already extinct by 1973 or because the assumption on which this prediction was based is false?" "Everyone expected that 'One Big Union'—the slogan of the movement—would strike and win wage increases for workers. Yet statistical evidence shows just the contrary: strong unions do not strike but instead restrain workers' wage demands."

It is often worthwhile to help readers understand how the research task grows from the intellectual history or current intellectual life of the country or region that generated it. Council committees strive to build linkages among an immense diversity of national and international intellectual traditions, and members come from various countries and schools of thought. Many committee members are interested in the interplay of diverse traditions. In fact, the chance to see intellectual history in the making is another reason people accept committee membership. It is a motive to which proposals can legitimately appeal.

It pays to remember that topics of current salience, both theoretical and in the so-called real world, are likely to be a crowded field. The competitors will be more numerous and the competition less interesting than in truly unfamiliar terrain. Unless you have something truly original to say about them, you may be well advised to avoid topics typically styled "of central interest to the discipline." Usually these are topics about which everyone is writing, and the reason is that somebody else has already made the decisive and exciting contribution. By the time you write your proposal, obtain funding, do the research, and write it up, you might wish you were working on something else. So if your instinct leads you to a problem far from the course that the pack is running, follow it—not the pack: nothing is more valuable than a really fresh beginning.

Describe Your Methodology

Methodological canons are largely discipline specific and vary widely even within some disciplines. But two things can safely be said about methodological appeal. First, the proposal must specify the research operations you will undertake and the way you will interpret the results of these operations in terms of your central problem. Do not just tell what you mean to achieve; tell how you will spend your time while doing it. Second, a methodology is not just a list of research tasks but an argument as to why these tasks add up to the best attack on the problem. An agenda by itself will normally not suffice because the mere listing of tasks to perform does not prove that they add up to the best feasible approach.

Some popularly used phrases fall short of identifying recognizable research operations. For example, "I will look at the relation between x and y" is not informative. We know what is meant when an ornithologist proposes to "look at" a bird, but "looking at" a relation between variables is something one only does indirectly, by operations like digging through dusty archive boxes, interviewing, observing and taking standardized notes, collecting and testing statistical patterns, etc. How will you tease the relationship of underlying forces from the mass of experience? The process of gathering data and moving from data to interpretation tends to follow disciplinary customs, more standard in some fields than in others; help readers from other fields recognize what parts of your methodology are standard, what innovative.

Be as specific as you possibly can be about the activities you plan to undertake to collect information, about the techniques you will use to analyze it, and about the tests of validity to which you commit yourself. Most proposals fail because they leave reviewers wondering what the applicant will actually do. Tell them! Specify the archives, the sources, the respondents, and the proposed techniques of analysis.

A research design proposing comparison between cases often has special appeal. In a certain sense all research is comparative because it must use, implicitly or explicitly, some point of reference. Making the comparison explicit raises its value as scientific inquiry. In evaluating a comparative proposal, readers ask whether the cases are chosen in such a way that their similarities and differences illuminate the central question. And is the proposer in a position to execute both legs of the comparison? When both answers are positive, the proposal may fare particularly well.

The proposal should prove that the researcher either possesses, or cooperates with people who possess, mastery of all the technical matters the project entails. For example, if a predominantly literary project includes an inquiry into the influence of the Tupian language on rural Brazilian Portuguese, the proposal will be checked for the author's background in linguistics and/or Indian languages, or the author's arrangements to collaborate with appropriate experts.

Specify Your Objectives

A well-composed proposal, like a sonata, usually ends by alluding to the original theme. How will research procedures and their products finally connect with the central question? How will you know if your idea was wrong or right? In some disciplines this imperative traditionally means holding to the strict canon of the falsifiable hypothesis. While respecting this canon, committee members are also open to less formal approaches. What matters is to convince readers that something is genuinely at stake in the inquiry—that it is not tendentiously moving toward a preconceived end—and that this leaven of the unknown will yield interesting, orderly propositions.

Proposals should normally describe the final product of the project: an article, book, chapter, dissertation, etc. If you have specific plans, it often helps to spell them out, because specifying the kind of journal in which you hope to publish, or the kind of people you hope to address, will help readers understand what might otherwise look like merely odd features of the proposal.

While planning and drafting your proposal, you should keep in mind the program guidelines and application procedures outlined in the brochure specific to the Council program to which you are applying. If you have specific questions about the program, you may wish to consult with a staff member. Your final proposal should include all requested enclosures and appendices.

Final Note

To write a good proposal takes a long time. Start early. Begin thinking about your topic well in advance and make it a habit to collect references while you work on other tasks. Write a first draft at least three months in advance, revise it, show it to colleagues. Let it gather a little dust, collect colleagues' comments, revise it again. If you have a chance, share it with a seminar or similar group; the debate should help you anticipate what reviewers will eventually think. Revise the text again for substance. Go over the language, style, and form. Resharpen your opening paragraph or first page so that it drives home exactly what you mean as effectively as possible.

Good luck.

Sample Curriculum Vitae

Jane Doe
1601 Pennsylvania Avenue, NW
Washington, DC 20016
(202) 555-1234

EDUCATION

1995 (exp.)	Ph.D., International Relations University of Columbia, Washington, DC, United States
1988	M.A., Political Science International College of War Studies, London, United Kingdom
1985	B.A., International Relations State University of New York, Albany, United States

DISSERTATION

"Ethnic Conflict in the Former Soviet Union: The Role of Conflict Management and Prevention"

FIELDS OF RESEARCH

International Relations, Peace Studies, Russian Area Studies, Women's Studies

EXPERIENCE

1992–1993	Research Assistant, Center for Peace Studies, University of Columbia
1990–1992	Research and Teaching Assistant, Department of Political Science, University of Columbia (Political Theory, International Relations, War in the 20th Century, Russian Government and Politics)
1989	Legislative and Research Assistant to Senator John Smith, United States Senate
1987–1988	Graduate Assistant, Centre for International Cooperation, International College of Defense Studies

HONORS AND AWARDS

1992–1993	Research Fellowship in the former Soviet Union, University of Columbia, U.S.-Russia Exchange Program
1992	Summer Language Institute Scholarship, Russian Language Institute, Moscow, Russia
1991	WIIS Summer Symposium for Graduate Students Participant
1991	Graduate Assistantship, Department of International Relations, University of Columbia
1990–1992	Graduate School Scholarship, University of Columbia
1988	Award for Master's Thesis

PUBLICATIONS AND PRESENTATIONS

"Russian Military Cutbacks: Figures and Meanings," Ch. 4 in *What Next for Russia? The Future of a Former Superpower,* eds. Hillary Johnson and Michael Stewart (New York: Wingate Hill, 1994): 102–125

"Prospects for Peace in the Former Soviet Union: A Forecast," paper presented at the International Security Studies Section/ISA-East annual conference, Washington, DC, 2–5 February 1993

"Boris Yeltsin and the Russian Military: Friends or Foes?" paper presented at the American Association for the Advancement of Slavic Studies annual conference, Atlanta, GA, 14–19 November 1992

LANGUAGES

Fluent Russian; Ukrainian reading proficiency

PROFESSIONAL MEMBERSHIPS

American Association for the Advancement of Slavic Studies

American Political Science Association

Women In International Security

Sample Cover Letter

Jane Doe
1601 Pennsylvania Avenue, NW
Washington, DC 20016

Dr. _____
Social Science Research Council
605 Third Avenue
New York, NY 10158

August 10, 1993

Dear Dr. _____ ,

Please accept my application for the SSRC-MacArthur Foundation Fellowship of Peace and Security in a Changing World. I first heard about your fellowship in the Women In International Security *Fellowships in International Affairs: A Guide to Opportunities in the United States and Abroad* and believe that my research interests and experience coincide perfectly with the goals and requirements of the fellowship. Enclosed please find my c.v., proposal, and list of references. I have asked recommenders to write to you directly.

I am currently pursuing a Ph.D. in international relations from the University of Columbia in Washington, DC. The topic of my dissertation is "Ethnic Conflict in the Former Soviet Union: The Role of Conflict Management and Prevention." With this work I hope to contribute not only to the understanding of the elements needed for effective peace-building but also to offer a unique interdisciplinary approach to conflict management. While considerable research has been done on the breakup of the Soviet Union and conflicts among emerging states, the role of crises prevention, negotiations, leadership training, and conflict management in creating regional stability has been virtually ignored. As a student of the former Soviet Union, I became aware that this is an area that needs further exploration. An abstract of my proposed dissertation is enclosed for your information.

SSRC support will allow me to write my dissertation in a timely manner and to contribute effectively to the understanding of the increasing ethnic conflict in the new states of the former Soviet Union. This is a very ambitious proposal, but I believe I am well prepared, both academically and professionally, to meet the challenges of the SSRC-MacArthur Fellowship. Without this support I will find it difficult to complete my work successfully.

Thank you very much for your consideration.

Sincerely,

Jane Doe

Attachments

Selected Bibliography of Other Fellowship Directories

Annual Register of Grant Support: A Directory of Funding Sources. 26th edition (New Providence: Bowker, 1993).

This general guide to grants and fellowships has special sections for "International Affairs and Area Studies," including subdivisions for international studies and research abroad, programs for foreign scholars, and technical assistance and cooperative research. There are additional divisions for political science and law.

Directory of Research Grants 1993 (Phoenix: Oryx, 1993).

This general guide lists grants and fellowships in the fields of international relations, international studies, international trade and finance, international and comparative law, and international organizations. Funding options are organized alphabetically by name of grant or fellowship.

Financial Aid for Research, Study, Travel, and Other Activities Abroad 1990–1991. Gael Ann Schlachter and R. David Weber (San Carlos: Reference Service Press, 1990).

This guide lists over 1,500 funding options from more than 550 organizations that sponsor research, study, travel, and other activities abroad. Funding is divided by academic level: high school and undergraduate; graduate; postdoctorate; professional and other individual. Listing is subdivided by type of activity: study, research, travel, or other. Indexes list grants by program title, sponsoring organization, geographic location, and subject.

Financial Resources for International Study. Institute of International Education (Princeton: Peterson's, 1989).

This general guide describes funding options for international study for all nationals.

Foundation Grants to Individuals. The Foundation Center. 8th edition (New York: Foundation Center, 1993).

This directory is designed specifically for individuals seeking grants or other financial opportunities. Six indexes divide the programs by subject area, type of support (scholarships, loans, or travel grants), geographic area, sponsoring company (for employee-restricted awards), educational institution (for grants limited to specific schools), and name of the foundation.

The Grants Register, 1993–1995. Lisa Williams, ed. (New York: St. Martin's, 1992).

A subject index assists in finding funding options for "Political Science and Government" programs. The register subdivides fellowships by region and substantive topics and lists grants for all nationals.

International Studies Funding and Resource Book: The Education Interface Guide to Sources of Support for International Education. Ginny Gutierrez and Ward Morehouse, eds. 5th edition (New York: Apex, 1990).

This book gives general information about international study funding programs, organized alphabetically by sponsoring organization.

Study Abroad. Vol. 27 (Paris: UNESCO, 1991).

This guide lists courses and scholarships for many programs outside the United States that are for scholars of all nationalities. The programs are organized alphabetically by country of origin.

INDEXES

Fellowships by Title

Abe Fellowship—Social Science Research Council

Academy for International and Area Studies Scholars Program—Center for International Affairs, Harvard University

Adenauer, Konrad, Fellowships—Konrad Adenauer Foundation

Advanced Research Fellowships—Center for International Affairs, Harvard University

Advanced Research Fellowship Programs—North Atlantic Treaty Organization

Advanced Seminar on the U.S. Foreign Policy Process—School of Public Affairs, University of Maryland at College Park

African Dissertation Internship Awards—Rockefeller Foundation

African Graduate Fellowships—American University in Cairo

Afro-American and African Studies Fellowship Programs—Carter G. Woodson Institute for Afro-American and African Studies, University of Virginia

AICGS/DHI Fellowships in Postwar German History—American Institute for Contemporary German Studies

American Fellowships—American Association of University Women Educational Foundation

American Studies—Japan–United States Friendship Commission

Annual Research Competition—National Council for Soviet and East European Research

ARCE Fellowships—American Research Center in Egypt, Inc.

Asian Foundation Fellowships—Asian Foundation

AUCC–Awards Division Programs—Association of Universities and Colleges of Canada

Barone, Joan Shorenstein, Congressional Fellowship—American Political Science Association

Bosch, Robert, Foundation Fellowship Program—Robert Bosch Foundation

Bosch Younger Scholar Program in the Social Sciences—American Institute for Contemporary German Studies

Bourse de l'Institut Européen des Hautes Etudes Internationales—Institut Européen des Hautes Etudes Internationales

Bourses Chateaubriand (Humanities)—Government of France
British Marshall Scholarships—Government of Great Britain
Bronfman, Edgar M., Fellowships for Economics in Eastern Europe—Institute of International Education
Bundeskanzler Scholarships for Future American Leaders—Alexander von Humboldt Foundation

Canadian Studies Faculty Enrichment Program—Canadian Studies Grant Programs
Canadian Studies Faculty Research Grant Program—Canadian Studies Grant Programs
Canadian Studies Graduate Student Fellowship Program—Canadian Studies Grant Programs
Canadian Studies Sabbatical Fellowship Program—Canadian Studies Grant Programs
Canadian Studies Senior Fellowship Award—Canadian Studies Grant Programs
Center for International Security and Arms Control Fellowships—Center for International Security and Arms Control, Stanford University
"Central and Eastern Europe" Academic Program: Grants for Junior Researchers—Volkswagen Foundation
China Conference Travel Grants—Committee on Scholarly Communications with China
China Times Cultural Foundation Scholarships
Chinese Fellowships for Scholarly Development—Committee on Scholarly Communications with China
Colombian Government Study and Research Grants—Government of Colombia
Conant, James Bryant, Fellowships for Postdoctoral Research—Center for European Studies, Harvard University
Congressional Fellowship Program: Communications—American Political Science Association
Congressional Fellowship Program: Federal Executives—American Political Science Association
Congressional Fellowship Program: Political Science—American Political Science Association
Congressional Fellowships on Women and Public Policy—Women's Research and Education Institute
Cullis, Winifred, Grants—International Federation of University Women

DAAD-AICGS Summer Grant—American Institute for Contemporary German Studies
Democratic Infrastructure Grants—Soros Foundations
Democratic Institutions Fellowship—North Atlantic Treaty Organization
Developmental Fellowships—International Research and Exchanges Board, Inc.
Directorate-General Information, Communication, Culture Programs—European Community

Dissertation Fellowship Competition—Institute for the Study of World Politics
Doctoral Fellowship—Japan Foundation
Doctoral Research Fellowships—Friedrich Ebert Foundation

Earhart Fellowship Research Grants—Earhart Foundation
East-West Center Fellows—East-West Center
East-West Center Graduate Degree Students Program—East-West Center
East-West Center Jefferson Fellowships—East-West Center
East-West Center Joint Predoctoral Research Fellowships—East-West Center
East-West Center Postdoctoral Fellowships—East-West Center
East-West Center Professional Associates Awards—East-West Center
EC-ASEAN Fellowship Programme (for citizens of ASEAN member states)—European Community
ECSA Dissertation Fellowships—European Community Studies Association
Eisenhower Exchange Fellowships
ERASMUS Bureau Programs—European Community
European Community's Visitors Programme—European Community
European Development Fund (for citizens of ACP countries)—European Community

Faculty Graduate Study Program for Historically Black Colleges and Universities—National Endowment for the Humanities
Fascell, Dante B., Inter-American Fellowship Program—Inter-American Foundation
Fellows Program—Albert Einstein Institution
Fellowship in National Security Studies—American Defense Institute
Fellowship Program to the People's Republic of China and the Former Soviet Union—International Education Center
Fellowship Programs—American Institute of Pakistan Studies
Fellowships and Grants for Study and Research—The American-Scandinavian Foundation
Fellowships for College Teachers and Independent Scholars—National Endowment for the Humanities
Fellowships for Senior Scholarly Development—American Institute of Indian Studies
Fellowships for University Professors—National Endowment for the Humanities
Fellowships/Grants-in-Aid—American Council of Learned Societies
Fellowships/Grants-in-Aid—Women in Government Relations Leader Foundation
Field Research Program at Master's/Doctoral Level—Inter-American Foundation
Fondation Franco-Américaine Fellowships—Fondation Franco-Américaine
Ford Foundation International Affairs Grants—Ford Foundation
Ford Foundation Postdoctoral Fellowship for Minorities—National Academy of Sciences, National Research Council

Foreign Language and Area Studies Fellowships—Center for Latin American Studies, University of Pittsburgh
Fulbright Program Award in Japan for U.S. Nationals—United States Information Agency
Fulbright Scholar Program—United States Information Agency

Gallatin, Albert, Fellowship in International Affairs—Foundation for Education and Research in International Studies
General Graduate Fellowships—Zeta Phi Beta Sorority National Education Foundation
German Historical Institute Scholarship—German Historical Institute
Graduate Exchange Fellowships—Belgian-American Educational Foundation, Inc.
Graduate Program—Committee on Scholarly Communications with China
Graduate Scholarships—Rotary Foundation
Grants/Fellowships—Business and Professional Women's Foundation
Guggenheim, Harry Frank, Foundation Grants—Harry Frank Guggenheim Foundation

Harkness Fellowship Program—Commonwealth Fund
Hopkins-Nanjing Program Scholarships—School of Advanced International Studies, Johns Hopkins University
Humboldt Research Awards for Foreign Scholars–Humanities Award—Alexander von Humboldt Foundation
Humboldt Research Fellowships for Foreign Scholars—Alexander von Humboldt Foundation
Humphrey, Hubert H., Doctoral Fellowships—Arms Control and Disarmament Agency, U.S.

IFUW Ida Smedley MacLean International Fellowships—International Federation of University Women
IHS Claude R. Lambe Fellowships—Institute for Humane Studies
Individual Advanced Research Opportunities for U.S. Scholars in Central and Eastern Europe—International Research and Exchanges Board, Inc.
Individual Advanced Research Opportunities for U.S. Scholars in Mongolia—International Research and Exchanges Board, Inc.
Individual Advanced Research Opportunities for U.S. Scholars in the States of the former Soviet Union—International Research and Exchanges Board, Inc.
Individual Advanced Research Opportunities in the United States for Mongolian Scholars—International Research and Exchanges Board, Inc.
Individual Advanced Research Opportunities in the United States for Scholars from Central and Eastern Europe and the Baltics—International Research and Exchanges Board, Inc.
Individual Advanced Research Opportunities in the United States for Scholars from the States of the Former Soviet Union—International Research and Exchanges Board, Inc.

International Affairs Fellowships—Council on Foreign Relations
International Fellowships—American Association of University Women Educational Foundation
International Human Rights Internship Program—Institute of International Education
International Peace and Security: Visiting Scholar Fellowships—Social Science Research Council
International Peace Scholarships—Rotary Foundation
International Predissertation Fellowship Program—Social Science Research Council
International Scholars Program—Joan B. Kroc Institute for International Peace Studies, University of Notre Dame
IRIS Research Program—Institutional Reform and the Informal Sector, University of Maryland

Japanese Studies—Japan–United States Friendship Commission
Javits, Jacob, Fellows Program—United States Department of Education
Johnson, Robert Wood, Health Policy Fellowship—American Political Science Association
Joint International Fellowship and Grant Programs for Area and Comparative Training and Research—Social Science Research Council
Junior (Dissertation) Fellowships—American Institute of Indian Studies

Kellogg, Helen, Institute for International Studies Residential Fellowships—Helen Kellogg Institute for International Studies, University of Notre Dame
Kellogg International Study Grant—W. K. Kellogg Foundation
Kennan Institute Research Scholarships—Kennan Institute for Advanced Russian Studies, Woodrow Wilson Center
Kennan Institute Short-Term Grants—Kennan Institute for Advanced Russian Studies, Woodrow Wilson Center
The Korea Foundation Fellowship for Korean-Language Training—Korea Foundation
The Korea Foundation Fellowship for Korean Studies—Korea Foundation

Leet, Dorothy, Grants—International Federation of University Women
Lentz, Theodore, Postdoctoral Fellowship in Global Issues, International Conflict and Peace—Center for International Studies, University of Missouri–St. Louis
Luce Scholars Program—Henry Luce Foundation, Inc.

MacArthur Fellows Program—The John D. and Catherine T. MacArthur Foundation
McNamara, Robert S., Fellowship Program—World Bank
Mexican Government Scholarships—Government of Mexico
Monbusho Scholarship (Research)—Government of Japan
Monnet, Jean, Fellowship—European University Institute

NAFSA China Study Missions—National Association for Foreign Student Affairs
National Fellowships—Hoover Institution on War, Revolution, and Peace
National Security Scholarships, Fellowships, and Grants—National Security Education Program, U.S. Department of Defense
NATO Research Grants in the Sciences—North Atlantic Treaty Organization
Naumann, Friedrich, Fellowships—Friedrich Naumann Foundation
Newcombe, Charlotte W., Doctoral Dissertation Fellowships—Woodrow Wilson National Fellowship Foundation
Norwegian Nobel Institute Fellowships—Norwegian Nobel Institute

OAS Regular Training Program—Organization of American States
Olin, John M., Fellowships in National Security/Economics and National Security—Center for International Affairs, Harvard University
OTA Congressional Fellowship Program—Office of Technology Assessment

Peace Fellowship—Mary Ingraham Bunting Institute of Radcliffe College
Pew Economic Freedom Fellows Program—Pew Trust Fellowship Programs
Pew Faculty Fellowship in International Affairs—Pew Trust Fellowship Programs
Planck, Max, Research Awards for Foreign and German Scholars—Alexander von Humboldt Foundation
Policy-Oriented Research—Japan–United States Friendship Commission
Postdoctoral Fellowship—Frederick Douglass Institute for African and African-American Studies, University of Rochester
Postdoctoral Fellowship for Research in International Security Studies—Mershon Center, Ohio State University
Postdoctoral Fellowship Program—Resources for the Future
Postdoctoral Fellowships—Harriman Institute for Advanced Study of the Soviet Union, Columbia University
Postdoctoral/Young Scholar Fellowships—Friedrich Ebert Foundation
Postgraduate Scholarships—European Free Trade Association
Pre- and Postdoctoral Fellowships—Center for International Affairs, Harvard University
Pre- and Postdoctoral Fellowships and Visiting Scholar Affiliations—Centers for International Affairs, Harvard University
Predissertation/Advanced Graduate Fellowships—Friedrich Ebert Foundation
Predissertation Fellowships—Council for European Studies, Colombia University
Presidential Management Internship Program—Presidential Management Internship Program, U.S. Office of Personnel Management
Program on Peace and International Cooperation—John D. and Catherine T. MacArthur Foundation

Randolph, Jennings, Program for International Peace—United States Institute of Peace

Research Contest—Centre for Transatlantic Foreign and Security Policy, Free University of Berlin
Research Fellowship—Japan Foundation
Research Fellowships—German Marshall Fund of the United States
Research Fellowships—Graduate Fellowships for Global Change, Oak Ridge Associated Universities
Research Fellowships—Saitama University, Institute for Policy Science
Research Fellowships for German Scholars—Alexander von Humboldt Foundation
Research Fellowships in Foreign Policy Studies—Brookings Institution
Research Grants for Recent Ph.D.'s and Ph.D. Candidates—German Academic Exchange Service
Research Program—Committee on Scholarly Communications with China
RFF Small Grants Program—Resources for the Future
Rhodes Scholarships—Rhodes Scholarship Trust
Rockefeller Foundation Social Science Research Fellowships in Agriculture and in Population Studies—Rockefeller Foundation
Rotary Grants for University Teachers to Serve in Developing Countries—Rotary Foundation
Rothmans Fellowships—Rothmans Foundation

SAIS and Bologna Center Fellowships—School of Advanced International Studies, Johns Hopkins University
Scholarship—School of Oriental and African Studies, University of London
Scholarships—China Times Cultural Foundation
Scholarships—European University
Scholarships for Sessions of Courses—Hague Academy of International Law
Scoville, Herbert, Peace Fellowship—Scoville Peace Fellowship Program
Seidel, Hanns, Fellowships—Hanns Seidel Foundation
Selected Professions Fellowships—American Association of University Women Educational Foundation
Senior (Postdoctoral) Research Fellowships—American Institute of Indian Studies
Small Grants Program—American Institute for Maghrib Studies, Johns Hopkins University
Social and Economic Science Division Research Projects—National Science Foundation
Solicited and Unsolicited Grants—United States Institute of Peace
Soros Scholarships and Fellowships—Soros Foundations
SSRC-MacArthur Foundation Fellowships on Peace and Security in a Changing World—Social Science Research Council
Staff Exchange Programs—Association of African Universities
Study Grants for College and University Teachers—National Endowment for the Humanities
Study Visit Research Grants for Faculty—German Academic Exchange Service

Summer Stipends—National Endowment for the Humanities
Supplementary Grants—Soros Foundations

Transatlantic Cooperation Program for Humanities Scholars—Alexander von Humboldt Foundation
Truman, Harry S., Research Institute for the Advancement of Peace Fellowships—The Hebrew University of Jerusalem

United Nations Institute for Training and Research Fellowships—United Nations
United States Graduate Study Program for Latin American and Caribbean Citizens—Inter-American Foundation

Visiting Scholars Program—Center on East-West Trade, Investment, and Communication, Duke University

Wallenberg, Raoul, Scholarships—The Hebrew University of Jerusalem
White House Fellowships—White House Fellows
Wilson, Woodrow, Center Fellowships—Woodrow Wilson International Center for Scholars
Woolridge, Nancy B., Fellowships—Zeta Phi Beta Sorority National Education Foundation
World Bank Graduate Scholarship Program—World Bank

Granting Organizations by Geographic Area of Specialization or Location

Africa

North Africa/Middle East

American Institute for Maghrib Studies, Johns Hopkins University
American Research Center in Egypt, Inc.
The Hebrew University of Jerusalem
Institute of International Education
Social Science Research Council

Sub-Saharan

American University in Cairo
Association of African Universities
Frederick Douglass Institute for African and African-American Studies, University of Rochester
Institute of International Education
W. K. Kellogg Foundation
Rockefeller Foundation
School of Oriental and African Studies, University of London
Social Science Research Council
Woodrow Wilson International Center for Scholars

Asia

East Asia

American Council of Learned Societies (with the Social Science Research Council)
Asian Foundation
Center for International Affairs, Harvard University
China Times Cultural Foundation

Committee on Scholarly Communications with China
East-West Center
Government of Japan
Institute of International Education
International Education Center
International Research and Exchanges Board, Inc.
Japan Foundation
Japan–United States Friendship Commission
Korea Foundation
Henry Luce Foundation, Inc.
National Association for Foreign Student Affairs
Saitama University, Institute for Policy Science
School of Advanced International Studies, Johns Hopkins University
School of Oriental and African Studies, University of London
Social Science Research Council
United States Information Agency
Woodrow Wilson International Center for Scholars

South Asia

American Institute of Indian Studies
American Institute of Pakistan Studies
Social Science Research Council

Australia

Institute of International Education
Rothmans Foundation

Canada

Association of Universities and Colleges of Canada
Canadian Studies Grant Programs

Europe (Eastern) and the Former Soviet Union

Center on East-West Trade, Investment, and Communication, Duke University
Harriman Institute for Advanced Study of the Soviet Union, Columbia University
Institute of International Education
International Education Center
International Research and Exchanges Board, Inc.
Kennan Institute for Advanced Russian Studies, Woodrow Wilson Center

National Council for Soviet and East European Research
Pew Trust Fellowship Programs
Social Science Research Council
Soros Foundations
Woodrow Wilson International Center for Scholars

Europe (Western)

General

Center for European Studies, Harvard University
Council for European Studies, Columbia University
European Community
European Community Studies Association
European Free Trade Association
Institute of International Education
North Atlantic Treaty Organization
Social Science Research Council
United Nations
Woodrow Wilson International Center for Scholars

Germany

Konrad Adenauer Foundation
American Institute for Contemporary German Studies
Robert Bosch Foundation
Centre for Transatlantic Foreign and Security Policy, Free University of Berlin
Friedrich Ebert Foundation
German Academic Exchange Service
German Historical Institute
German Marshall Fund of the United States
Alexander von Humboldt Foundation
Friedrich Naumann Foundation
Hanns Seidel Foundation
Volkswagen Foundation

United Kingdom

Commonwealth Fund
Government of Great Britain

France

European University
Fondation Franco-Américaine

Government of France
Institut Européen des Hautes Etudes Internationales

Scandinavia

American-Scandinavian Foundation
Norwegian Nobel Institute

Switzerland

Foundation for Education and Research in International Studies

Italy

European University Institute
School of Advanced International Studies, Johns Hopkins University

Belgium

Belgian-American Education Foundation, Inc.

Latin America/Caribbean

Center for Latin American Studies, University of Pittsburgh
Center for U.S.-Mexican Studies, University of California, San Diego
Government of Colombia
Institute of International Education
Inter-American Foundation
Helen Kellogg Institute for International Studies, University of Notre Dame
W. K. Kellogg Foundation
Government of Mexico
Organization of American States
Social Science Research Council
United States Institute of Peace
Woodrow Wilson International Center for Scholars

United States

American Association of University Women Educational Foundation
American Defense Institute
American Political Science Association
Arms Control and Disarmament Agency, U.S.

Institute of International Education
Mershon Center, Ohio State University
Office of Technology Assessment
Presidential Management Internship Program, U.S. Office of Personnel Management
School of Public Affairs, University of Maryland
Scoville Peace Fellowship Program
White House Fellows
Woodrow Wilson International Center for Scholars
Women In Government Relations Leader Foundation
Women's Research and Education Institute

Granting Organizations by Fellowship Type

Programs at Graduate/Dissertation Stage

Konrad Adenauer Foundation
American Association of University Women Educational Foundation—American Fellowships
American Association of University Women Educational Foundation—Selected Professions Fellowships
American Defense Institute—Fellowship in National Security Studies
American Institute for Contemporary German Studies—DAAD-AICGS Summer Grant
American Institute for Maghrib Studies, Johns Hopkins University—Small Grants Program
American Institute of Indian Studies—Junior (Dissertation) Fellowships
American Institute of Pakistan Studies—Fellowship Programs
American Political Science Association—Congressional Fellowship Programs
American Research Center in Egypt, Inc.—ARCE Fellowships
American University in Cairo—African Graduate Fellowships
American-Scandinavian Foundation—Fellowships and Grants for Study and Research
Arms Control and Disarmament Agency, U.S.—Hubert H. Humphrey Doctoral Fellowship
Association of Universities and Colleges of Canada—AUCC-Awards Division Programs
Belgian-American Educational Foundation, Inc.—Graduate Exchange Fellowships
Robert Bosch Foundation—Robert Bosch Foundation Fellowship Program
Brookings Institution—Research Fellowships in Foreign Policy Studies
Business and Professional Women's Foundation—Grants/Fellowships
Canadian Studies Grant Programs—Canadian Studies Graduate Student Fellowship Program
Center for International Affairs, Harvard University—Academy for International and Area Studies Scholars Program

Center for International Affairs, Harvard University—John M. Olin Fellowships in National Security/Economics and National Security
Center for International Affairs, Harvard University—Pre- and Postdoctoral Fellowships and Visiting Scholar Affiliations
Center for International Affairs, Harvard University—Pre- and Postdoctoral Fellowships
Center for International Security and Arms Control—Center for International Security and Arms Control Fellowships
Center for Latin American Studies, University of Pittsburgh—Foreign Language and Area Studies Fellowships
Center for U.S.-Mexican Studies, University of California, San Diego—Visiting Research Fellowships
Center on East-West Trade, Investment, and Communication, Duke University—Visiting Scholars Program
Centre for Transatlantic Foreign and Security Policy, Free University of Berlin—Research Contest
China Times Cultural Foundation—Scholarships
Government of Colombia—Colombian Government Study and Research Grants
Committee on Scholarly Communications with China—Graduate Program
Commomwealth Fund—The Harkness Fellowship Program
Council for European Studies—Predissertation Fellowships
Earhart Foundation—Earhart Fellowship Research Grants
East-West Center—East-West Center Graduate Degree Students Program
East-West Center—East-West Center Joint Predoctoral Research Fellowships
Friedrich Ebert Foundation—Doctoral Research Fellowships
Friedrich Ebert Foundation—Predissertation/Advanced Graduate Fellowships
Albert Einstein Institution—Fellows Program
European Community Studies Association—ECSA Dissertation Fellowships
Foundation for Education and Research in International Studies—Albert Gallatin Fellowship in International Affairs
Government of France—Bourses Chateaubriand (Humanities)
German Academic Exchange Service—Research Grants for Recent Ph.D.'s and Ph.D. Candidates
German Historical Institute—German Historical Institute Scholarship
Graduate Fellowships for Global Change—Research Fellowships
Government of Great Britain—British Marshall Scholarships
Harry Frank Guggenheim Foundation—Harry Frank Guggenheim Foundation Grants
The Hebrew University—The Raoul Wallenberg Scholarships
Institute for Humane Studies—IHS Claude R. Lambe Fellowships
Institute for the Study of World Politics—Dissertation Fellowship Competition
Institute of International Education—Edgar M. Bronfman Fellowships for Economics in Eastern Europe
Institute of International Education—International Human Rights Internship Program

Inter-American Foundation—Field Research Program at Master's/Doctoral Level
International Federation of University Women—The IFUW Ida Smedley MacLean International Fellowships
International Federation of University Women—The Winifred Cullis Grants
International Research and Exchanges Board, Inc.—Developmental Fellowships
International Research and Exchanges Board, Inc.—Individual Advanced Research Opportunities for U.S. Scholars in Central and Eastern Europe
International Research and Exchanges Board, Inc.—Individual Advanced Research Opportunities for U.S. Scholars in Mongolia
International Research and Exchanges Board, Inc.—Individual Advanced Research Opportunities for U.S. Scholars in the States of the Former Soviet Union
Government of Japan—Monbusho Scholarship (Research)
The Japan Foundation—Doctoral Fellowship
Japan-United States Friendship Commission—Japanese Studies
Kennan Institute for Advanced Russian Studies—Kennan Institute Short-Term Grants
Korea Foundation—The Korea Foundation Fellowship for Korean-Language Training
Korea Foundation—The Korea Foundation Fellowship for Korean Studies
Government of Mexico—Mexican Government Scholarships
National Endowment for the Humanities—Faculty Graduate Study Program for Historically Black Colleges and Universities
Friedrich Naumann Foundation
Presidential Management Internship Program—Presidential Management Internship Program
Rhodes Scholarship Trust—Rhodes Scholarships
Rotary Foundation—Graduate Scholarships
School of Advanced International Studies, Johns Hopkins University—Hopkins-Nanjing Program Scholarships
School of Advanced International Studies, Johns Hopkins University—SAIS and Bologna Center Fellowships
School of Oriental and African Studies, University of London—Scholarship
Hanns Seidel Foundation
Social Science Research Council—SSRC-MacArthur Foundation Fellowships of Peace and Security in a Changing World
Social Science Research Council—International Predissertation Fellowship Program
Social Science Research Council—Joint International Fellowship and Grant Programs for Area and Comparative Training and Research
Soros Foundations—Soros Scholarships and Fellowships
United States Department of Education—Jacob Javits Fellows Program
United States Information Agency—Fulbright Program Award in Japan for U.S. Nationals

United States Institute of Peace—Jennings Randolph Program for International Peace
Woodrow Wilson National Fellowship Foundation—Charlotte W. Newcombe Doctoral Dissertation Fellowships
Women's Research and Education Institute—Congressional Fellowships on Women and Public Policy
Carter G. Woodson Institute for Afro-American and African Studies, University of Virginia—Afro-American and African Studies Fellowship Programs
World Bank—World Bank Graduate Scholarship Program
Zeta Phi Beta Sorority National Education Foundation—General Graduate Fellowships
Zeta Phi Beta Sorority National Education Foundation—Nancy B. Woolridge Fellowships

Programs at Postdoctoral Stage

American Association of University Women Educational Foundation—American Fellowships
American Council of Learned Societies—Fellowships/Grants-in-Aid
American Institute for Contemporary German Studies—AICGS/DHI Fellowships in Postwar German History
American Institute for Contemporary German Studies—DAAD-AICGS Summer Grant
American Institute for Contemporary German Studies—Bosch Younger Scholar Program in the Social Sciences
American Institute of Indian Studies—Senior (Postdoctoral) Research Fellowships
American Institute of Pakistan Studies—Fellowship Programs
American Political Science Association—Congressional Fellowship Program: Communications
American Political Science Association—Congressional Fellowship Program: Political Science
American Research Center in Egypt, Inc.—ARCE Fellowships
Canadian Studies Grant Programs—Canadian Studies Faculty Enrichment Program
Canadian Studies Grant Programs—Canadian Studies Faculty Research Grant Program
Canadian Studies Grant Programs—Canadian Studies Sabbatical Fellowship Program
Canadian Studies Grant Programs—Canadian Studies Senior Fellowship Award
Center for European Studies, Harvard University—James Bryant Conant Fellowships for Postdoctoral Research
Center for International Affairs, Harvard University—Academy for International and Area Studies Scholars Program

Center for International Affairs, Harvard University—Advanced Research Fellowships
Center for International Affairs, Harvard University—John M. Olin Fellowships in National Security/Economics and National Security
Center for International Affairs, Harvard University—Pre- and Postdoctoral Fellowships
Center for International Affairs, Harvard University—Pre- and Postdoctoral Fellowships and Visiting Scholar Affiliations
Center for International Security and Arms Control—Center for International Security and Arms Control Fellowships
Center for International Studies, University of Missouri–St. Louis—Theodore Lentz Postdoctoral Fellowship in Global Issues, International Conflict and Peace Research
Center for U.S.-Mexican Studies, University of California, San Diego—Visiting Research Fellowships
Center on East-West Trade, Investment, and Communication, Duke University—Visiting Scholars Program
Committee on Scholarly Communications with China—China Conference Travel Grants
Committee on Scholarly Communications with China—Research Program
Council on Foreign Relations—International Affairs Fellowships
Frederick Douglass Institute for African and African-American Studies, University of Rochester—Postdoctoral Fellowship
East-West Center—East-West Center Postdoctoral Fellowships
Friedrich Ebert Foundation—Postdoctoral/Young Scholar Fellowships
Albert Einstein Institution—Fellows Program
European Community—European Community's Visitors Programme
European Free Trade Association—Postgraduate Scholarships
European University Institute—Jean Monnet Fellowship
Government of France—Bourses Chateaubriand (Humanities)
German Academic Exchange Service—Research Grants for Recent Ph.D's and Ph.D. Candidates
German Academic Exchange Service—Study Visit Research Grants for Faculty
German Marshall Fund of the United States—Research Fellowships
Harry Frank Guggenheim Foundation—Harry Frank Guggenheim Foundation Grants
Harriman Institute for Advanced Study of the Soviet Union, Columbia University—Postdoctoral Fellowships
The Hebrew University—The Harry S. Truman Research Institute for the Advancement of Peace
Hoover Institution on War, Revolution, and Peace—National Fellowships
Alexander von Humboldt Foundation—Humboldt Research Awards for Foreign Scholars–Humanities Award
Alexander von Humboldt Foundation—Humboldt Research Fellowships for Foreign Scholars

Institut Européen des Hautes Etudes Internationales—Bourse de l'Institut Européen des Hautes Etudes Internationales

International Research and Exchanges Board, Inc.—Developmental Fellowships

International Research and Exchanges Board, Inc.—Individual Advanced Research Opportunities for U.S. Scholars in Central and Eastern Europe

International Research and Exchanges Board, Inc.—Individual Advanced Research Opportunities for U.S. Scholars in Mongolia

International Research and Exchanges Board, Inc.—Individual Advanced Research Opportunities for U.S. Scholars in the States of the Former Soviet Union

Helen Kellogg Institute for International Studies, University of Notre Dame—Helen Kellogg Institute for International Studies Residential Fellowships

Kennan Institute for Advanced Russian Studies, Woodrow Wilson Center—Kennan Institute Research Scholarships

Kennan Institute for Advanced Russian Studies, Woodrow Wilson Center—Kennan Institute Short-Term Grants

Korea Foundation—The Korea Foundation Fellowship for Korean Studies

Korea Foundation—The Korea Foundation Fellowship for Korean-Language Training

Mershon Center, Ohio State University—Postdoctoral Fellowship for Research in International Security Studies

National Academy of Science, National Research Council—Ford Foundation Postdoctoral Fellowship for Minorities

National Council for Soviet and East European Research—Annual Research Competition

North Atlantic Treaty Organization—Advanced Research Fellowship Programs

North Atlantic Treaty Organization—NATO Research Grants in the Sciences

Office of Technology Assessment—OTA Congressional Fellowship Program

Pew Trust Fellowship Programs—Pew Faculty Fellowship in International Affairs

Resources for the Future—Postdoctoral Fellowship Program

Rockefeller Foundation—Rockefeller Foundation Social Science Research Fellowships in Agriculture and in Population Studies

Rotary Foundation—Rotary Grants for University Teachers to Serve in Developing Countries

Rothmans Foundation—Rothmans Fellowships

Saitama University, Institute for Policy Science—Research Fellowships

School of Advanced International Studies, Johns Hopkins University—Hopkins-Nanjing Program Scholarships

Social Science Research Council—SSRC-MacArthur Foundation Fellowships on Peace and Security in a Changing World

Social Science Research Council—Joint International Fellowship and Grant Programs for Area and Comparative Training and Research
United States Information Agency—Fulbright Program Award in Japan for U.S. Nationals
United States Information Agency—Fulbright Scholar Program
United States Institute of Peace—Jennings Randolph Program for International Peace
Volkswagen Foundation—"Central and Eastern Europe" Academic Program: Grants for Junior Researchers
Woodrow Wilson International Center for Scholars—Woodrow Wilson Center Fellowships
Carter G. Woodson Institute for Afro-American and African Studies, University of Virginia—Afro-American and African Studies Fellowship Programs
World Bank—Robert S. McNamara Fellowships Program

Qualifications Not Specified/ Professional Experience Alternative

American Institute of Indian Studies—Fellowships for Senior Scholarly Development
American Political Science Association—Congressional Fellowship Program: Federal Executives
American Political Science Association—Joan Shorenstein Barone Congressional Fellowship
American Political Science Association—Robert Wood Johnson Health Policy Fellowship
Asian Foundation—Asian Foundation Fellowships
Robert Bosch Foundation—Robert Bosch Foundation Fellowship Program
Mary Ingraham Bunting Institute of Radcliffe College—Peace Fellowship
Council on Foreign Relations—International Affairs Fellowships
East-West Center—East-West Center Fellows
East-West Center—East-West Center Jefferson Fellowships
East-West Center—East-West Center Professional Associates Awards
Albert Einstein Institution—Fellows Program
Eisenhower Exchange Fellowships
European Community—EC-ASEAN Fellowship Programme (for citizens of ASEAN member states)
European Community—European Community's Visitors Programme
European Community—European Development Fund (for citizens of ACP countries)
Fondation Franco-Américaine—Fondation Franco-Américaine Fellowships
Ford Foundation—Ford Foundation International Affairs Grants
Hague Academy of International Law—Scholarships for Sessions of Courses

Alexander von Humboldt Foundation—Bundeskanzler Scholarships
Institutional Reform and the Informal Sector, University of Maryland—IRIS Research Program
International Education Center—Fellowship Program to the People's Republic of China and the Former Soviet Union
International Federation of University Women—Dorothy Leet Grants
Japan Foundation—Research Fellowship
Japan–United States Friendship Commission—Policy-Oriented Research
Kennan Institute for Advanced Russian Studies, Woodrow Wilson Center—Kennan Institute Short-Term Grants
Korea Foundation—The Korea Foundation Fellowship for Korean-Language Training
John D. and Catherine T. MacArthur Foundation—Program on Peace and International Cooperation
National Association for Foreign Student Affairs—NAFSA China Study Missions
National Council for Soviet and East European Research—Annual Research Competition
National Endowment for the Humanities—Fellowships for College Teachers and Independent Scholars
National Endowment for the Humanities—Fellowships for University Professors
National Endowment for the Humanities—Study Grants for College and University Teachers
National Endowment for the Humanities—Summer Stipends
National Science Foundation—Social and Economic Science Division Research Projects
National Security Education Program, U.S. Department of Defense—National Security Scholarships, Fellowships, and Grants
Norwegian Nobel Institute—Norwegian Nobel Institute Fellowships
Resources for the Future—The RFF Small Grants Program
Rotary Foundation—International Peace Scholarships
School of Advanced International Studies, Johns Hopkins University—Hopkins-Nanjing Program Scholarships
School of Public Affairs, University of Maryland—Advanced Seminar on the U.S. Foreign Policy Process
Social Science Research Council—Abe Fellowship
Soros Foundations—Democratic Infrastructure Grants
United States Information Agency—Fulbright Program Award in Japan for U.S. Nationals
United States Institute of Peace—Jennings Randolph Program for International Peace
United States Institute of Peace—Solicited and Unsolicited Grants Program
White House Fellows—White House Fellowships
Woodrow Wilson International Center for Scholars—Woodrow Wilson Center Fellowships
Women in Government Relations Leader Foundation—Fellowships/Grants-in-Aid

Programs at Undergraduate Stage

China Times Cultural Foundation—Scholarships
European University—Scholarships
Institute for Humane Studies, George Mason University—IHS Claude R. Lambe Fellowships
Korea Foundation—The Korea Foundation Fellowship for Korean-Language Training
Henry Luce Foundation, Inc.—Luce Scholars
Scoville Peace Fellowship Program—Herbert Scoville Peace Fellowship
University of Maryland, College Park—Scholarships for Adult Women

Programs Available to Non-U.S. Applicants

Konrad Adenauer Foundation
American Association of University Women Educational Foundation—International Fellowships
American Council of Learned Societies—German-American Collaborative Research Grants in the Humanities and Social Sciences
American Institute for Contemporary German Studies—AICGS/DHI Fellowships in Postwar German History
American Political Science Association—Congressional Fellowship Program: Communications
American Research Center in Egypt, Inc.—ARCE Fellowships
American University in Cairo—African Graduate Fellowships
Asian Foundation—Asian Foundation Fellowships
Centre for Transatlantic Foreign and Security Policy, Free University of Berlin—Research Contest
Committee on Scholarly Communications with China—Chinese Fellowships for Scholarly Development
Commonwealth Fund—Harkness Fellowship Program
Friedrich Ebert Foundation
European Community—EC-ASEAN Fellowship Programme (for citizens of ASEAN member states)
European Community—European Development Fund (for citizens of ACP countries)
European Community—European Community's Visitors Programme
Fondation Franco-Américaine—Fondation Franco-Américaine Fellowships
The Hebrew University—The Harry S. Truman Research Institute for the Advancement of Peace
Alexander von Humboldt Foundation—Humboldt Research Fellowships for Foreign Scholars
Alexander von Humboldt Foundation—Humboldt Research Awards for Foreign Scholars–Humanities Award
Alexander von Humboldt Foundation—Max Planck Research Awards for Foreign and German Scholars

Alexander von Humboldt Foundation—Transatlantic Cooperation Program for Humanities Scholars
Institut Européen des Hautes Etudes Internationales—Bourse de l'Institut Européen des Hautes Etudes Internationales
Institute for Humane Studies, George Mason University—IHS Claude R. Lambe Fellowships
Institute for the Study of World Politics—Dissertation Fellowship Competition
Inter-American Foundation—Dante B. Fascell Inter-American Fellowship Program
Inter-American Foundation—U.S. Graduate Study Program for Latin American and Caribbean Citizens
International Federation of University Women—IFUW Ida Smedley MacLean International Fellowships
International Federation of University Women—Winifred Cullis Grants
International Federation of University Women—Dorothy Leet Grants
International Research and Exchanges Board, Inc.—Individual Advanced Research Opportunities in the United States for Mongolian Scholars
International Research and Exchanges Board, Inc.—Individual Advanced Research Opportunities in the United States for Scholars from Central and Eastern Europe and the Baltics
International Research and Exchanges Board, Inc.—Individual Advanced Research Opportunities in the United States for Scholars from the States of the Former Soviet Union
Government of Japan—Monbusho Scholarship
Japan–United States Friendship Commission—American Studies
W. K. Kellogg Foundation—Kellogg International Study Grant
Korea Foundation—The Korea Foundation Fellowship for Korean-Language Training
Korea Foundation—The Korea Foundation Fellowship for Korean Studies
Joan B. Kroc Institute for International Peace Studies, University of Notre Dame—International Scholars Program
John D. and Catherine T. MacArthur Foundation—MacArthur Fellows Program
John D. and Catherine T. MacArthur Foundation—Program on Peace and International Cooperation
Friedrich Naumann Foundation
North Atlantic Treaty Organization—Advanced Research Fellowship Programs
North Atlantic Treaty Organization—NATO Research Grants in the Sciences
Norwegian Nobel Institute—Norwegian Nobel Institute Fellowships
Organization of American States—OAS Regular Training Program
Pew Trust Fellowship Programs—Pew Economic Freedom Fellows Program
Resources for the Future—Postdoctoral Fellowship Program
Rhodes Scholarship Trust—Rhodes Scholarships

Rockefeller Foundation—African Dissertation Internship Awards
Rotary Foundation—Graduate Scholarships
Rotary Foundation—International Peace Fellowships
Rotary Foundation—Rotary Grants for University Teachers to Serve in Developing Countries
Rothmans Foundation—Rothmans Fellowships
Saitama University, Institute for Policy Science—Research Fellowships
Hanns Seidel Foundation
School of Public Affairs, University of Maryland—Advanced Seminar on the U.S. Foreign Policy Process
Social Science Research Council—Abe Fellowship
Social Science Research Council—International Peace and Security: Visiting Scholar Fellowships
Soros Foundations—Soros Scholarships and Fellowships
United States Information Agency—Fulbright Scholar Program
United States Institute of Peace—Jennings Randolph Program for International Peace
Volkswagen Foundation—"Central and Eastern Europe" Academic Program: Grants for Junior Researchers
Carter G. Woodson Institute for Afro-American and African Studies, University of Virginia—Afro-American and African Studies Fellowship Programs
World Bank—Robert S. McNamara Fellowships Program
World Bank—World Bank Graduate Scholarship Program
Zeta Phi Beta Sorority National Education Foundation—Nancy B. Woolridge Fellowships

About Women In International Security

THE UNITED STATES faces a multitude of foreign policy challenges. Experienced and talented individuals drawn from all areas of national life must be available if wise choices are to be made. Yet in the past, women have not generally been among those asked to contribute their skills. In effect, 50 percent of the available talent has been excluded from the pool of individuals who will deal with the most vital issues facing us today.

But there are some positive signs. In the past ten years, the percentage of doctorates awarded to women in international relations has doubled, and during the past six years, about one-third of those entering the U.S. diplomatic corps have been women. More women are entering the graduate schools and professional programs that lead to effective membership in the policy community. The next few years will be critical if women are to advance to influential policymaking and research positions in significant numbers.

Founded by Catherine McArdle Kelleher in 1987, Women In International Security is an international, nonpartisan network and educational program dedicated to enhancing opportunities for women working in the field of international security. The program involves women in the military, government, in policymaking and diplomatic areas, the media, and academia.

WIIS (pronounced "wise") is designed to enable women to fulfill their career expectations. We hope not only to increase the number of women working as international security professionals but also to enhance the prospects of those already in the field, especially at beginning and midcareer levels. WIIS provides women currently working in international security, as well as those considering it as a career, with a structure of informal links and continuing career contacts. This structure rests on a foundation of specific activities, including:

- WIIS databank—a computerized listing that is used to match women and professional opportunities
- WIIS directories—of which this is the second, following an earlier directory on internships in foreign and defense policy
- *WIIS Words*—a quarterly newsletter
- WIIS seminars and conferences—meetings that present networking opportunities and substantive discussions
- WIIS Summer Symposium on International Security for Graduate Students—an annual program of expert panel discussions on a specific topic and professional development workshops
- WIIS international partnerships and collaborative programs—a joint effort on ethnic conflict in Eastern Europe and the former Soviet Union with Women In Global Security (WINGS) based in Moscow

WIIS is funded by the Ford Foundation, the Carnegie Corporation of New York, other private and public donors, and its membership. It is based at the Center for International and Security Studies located at the School of Public Affairs on the College Park campus of the University of Maryland. The executive director of WIIS is Carola Weil.

Women In International Security

Advisory Board

Beverly B. Byron
Anne H. Cahn
Jacquelyn K. Davis
Evelyn P. Foote
Georgie Anne Geyer
Nancy Landon Kassebaum
Betty Goetz Lall
Claire E. Max
Elizabeth Pond

Judith V. Reppy
Rozanne L. Ridgway
Enid C. B. Schoettle
Harriet Fast Scott
Mady Wechsler Segal
Jane M. O. Sharp
Angela Stent
Mitzi M. Wertheim

Executive Board

Yvonne M. Bartoli
Susan J. Bennett
Ellen S. Blalock
Avis T. Bohlen
Sheila R. Buckley
Natalie J. Goldring
Rose Gottemoeller,
  ex officio
Carol Rae Hansen
Margaret A. Harlow

Laurie C. Hoes
Jo L. Husbands
Sharon P. Jackson
Catherine McArdle Kelleher
Lousie Lief
Gale A. Mattox
Johanna S. R. Mendelson
Patricia M. Ravalgi
Lynn F. Rusten
Patricia Stein Wrightson

For further information contact:
Women In International Security
Center for International and Security Studies
School of Public Affairs
University of Maryland
College Park, MD 20742
(301) 405-7612
FAX: (301) 403-8107
E-mail: wiis@puafmail.umd.edu

About the Center for International and Security Studies at Maryland

The Center for International and Security Studies at Maryland (CISSM) works to enhance research, training, and policy-oriented scholarship across a wide range of international issues. Founded in 1985 as the Maryland International Security Project, CISSM is based at the School of Public Affairs at the University of Maryland at College Park. The center fosters research by students and scholars in a variety of disciplines, including political science, sociology, economics, and public affairs. It sponsors numerous activities, such as conferences, lectures, and publications.

Current research programs at CISSM focus on three areas: building cooperative security in the new post–Cold War era, with a special focus on multilateral conflict management and arms control; managing complex interdependence among advanced industrial nations, particularly the United States, Japan, and Europe; and reforming the foreign policy process to respond to the new global challenges facing the United States.

In addition to Women In International Security, several other major programs are associated with the center. The Rethinking Arms Control project sponsors discussion groups and publications intended to challenge basic assumptions of past arms control efforts and existing military arguments. The Maryland Seminar on the Foreign Policy Process provides fifteen to twenty foreign policy professionals with five months of intensive academic training and practical exposure to the making of U.S. policy on international security and economic questions.

The director of CISSM is I. M. Destler, the executive director is Frances G. Burwell, and the director of research is Ivo H. Daalder. For further information, contact:

CISSM/School of Public Affairs
University of Maryland
College Park, MD 20742
(301) 405-7601/FAX: (301) 403-8107

Fellowship Update Form

Women In International Security would like to continue to update this directory. If you have any suggestions or information about fellowships or grant programs that should be included, please fill out the form below with the appropriate information. Thank you for your assistance.

    Please send all fellowship information to:
        Women In International Security
        Center for International and Security Studies at Maryland
        School of Public Affairs
        University of Maryland
        College Park, MD 20742
        attn: FIA Guide
        (301) 405-7612
        FAX: (301) 403-8107

Fellowship Name: _____

Sponsoring Organization/Institution: _____

Description: _____

_____

_____

Qualifications: _____

Deadline: _____

Duration: _____

Amount: _____

Contact: _____

Address: _____

_____

_____

Phone/FAX: _____

Additional Information: _____

Date of Information: _____